Life, Death,
and Somewhere
In Between

Life, Death, and Somewhere In Between

*Observations on These and
Other Experiences As Seen through My Eyes*

JEFF HIELKEMA

authorHOUSE®

AuthorHouse™
1663 Liberty Drive
Bloomington, IN 47403
www.authorhouse.com
Phone: 1-800-839-8640

Published by AuthorHouse   08/20/2012

ISBN: 978-1-4772-6120-0 (sc)
ISBN: 978-1-4772-6119-4 (hc)
ISBN: 978-1-4772-6118-7 (e)

Library of Congress Control Number: 2012914816

There is no greater joy in life than the birth of a child.
There is no greater sorrow in life than to have to bury that child.
—Me, 2006

This book is dedicated to three women who have greatly impacted my life through their lives, and unfortunately, two through their deaths. I love them all deeply and cherish their memories.

Ma Sue: I always looked up to you, even though you were a full foot shorter than me. You not only gave me life, you were always there for me, even when I didn't realize or appreciate it. I could not have asked for a better mother. I love you and miss you terribly.

Stormi Liz: I still struggle with day-to-day life without you. I hope these writings will do your life justice, and in some way, ease some of the pain of losing you. I miss and love you more than words can say.

Jamie Rae: You taught me more about "life" and "strength" in a three-week period than most of us learn in a lifetime. As I said after your accident, "Jamie, when I grow up, I want to be just like you." I would never have thought it was possible, but I love you more than ever.

Foreword

It goes without saying that life isn't always fair. But then, who decides what is and what isn't fair? One person's idea of "fair" or "unfair" might be completely different from another's. Some might even think that when events happen, there isn't anything fair or unfair about it, it's just "life." Some people get dealt a lot of events throughout their lives, others just a few or none at all. This is the story of events in my life thus far, fair or unfair. In my eyes, some of it has been more than fair; some of it has been very unfair. I'll let you decide . . .

I had actually started on this project back in the first month or two of 2009. I type slowly (a two-finger speed demon) and sometimes "think" just as slowly. I type a paragraph or two and then sit back, read, and reread it to see if the words ended up on paper the same way the thoughts were arranged in my head. Later I edit again as I think of other things I want to say or feelings I had/have. In other words, it's a slow process.

I had started on the "somewhere in between" and "death" parts of the book simply because I wanted to write some of my thoughts and feelings. It wasn't necessarily meant to be a book or to be titled as such. If nothing else, it was therapy for me, a way to vent a little. Over the summer months I hardly even looked at any of it. Then on September 9, 2009, "life" happened. Shortly after that, the "lightbulb" in my head started to flicker. Things, life—whatever you want to call it—had come full circle, and the three parts all tied together. Now it's a passion, a must for me to finish. It's still a slow process, but I'm getting there.

I am not by any means an author. I'm just a guy writing his feelings down. I have never come close to writing a book before. And based on my reasons for this one, I hope to never write another. I do not have a degree or certificate of any kind that qualifies me to give advice on how to handle grief. What I do have is the Death Certificate for one of my children. That certificate more than qualifies me to write on the meaning of grief.

This book is simply a writing of observations and experiences from my life and from the lives of my daughters as seen through my eyes. It is, unfortunately, also about observations and experiences from the death of one of my daughters. For those of you who have had to bury a child, you know there is nothing worse. It is also about the death of my mother. A person may not think about it on a daily basis, but in the back of your mind you know chances are pretty good that at some point in time you will bury your parents. Knowing that doesn't make it any easier. To make matters worse, their deaths were fewer than eight weeks apart. Part of this book is about those terrible experiences.

There may be times in life when something terrible happens to one of your children and great things come out of it. The outcome is much better than what it could (or should) have been. Such is the case for one of my daughters, and part of this book is about those terrible-turned-not-so-terrible experiences.

Occasionally during life's journey, something happens to yourself that forever changes you and the way you look at things/ life. In my case, the event causing the changes made it easier to deal with, or live thorough, some events later in life. Again, that's part of what this book is about.

Sometimes it all ties together. There may be those who won't see some of the "ties" the same way I do, and that's fine; we don't all look at things in the same manner. Again, these are observations of experiences, good and bad, as seen through my eyes.

Part of what follows are my thoughts on grief. Grief comes in many shapes and forms and can ruin lives, relationships, and cause deep depression. Part of what this book is about is how I handle grief and what I do to keep my *chin up*.

If anyone can take something useful from any of my thoughts, that's wonderful. You never know. A way I handled or looked at something may work for others as well. I'm not trying to tell anyone what to do, only telling what worked/works for me.

If you get nothing else from this book, I hope you at least enjoy "meeting" my daughters (and my parents). Like any other parent, I love my children deeply and have an overabundance of pride for them.

History Lesson

S ometimes you need a brief history about people in order to understand who they are and why they are the way they are. In order to see where you're going, you have to see where you've been. This is my "history." I'll try to keep it from getting too boring. Here goes.

I was born in 1960 to Wisconsin dairy farmers, Harvey and Suzanna (Sue). Mom and Dad got married in 1958 when Mom was seventeen and Dad was twenty-three. Mom's parents had told her she couldn't get married until she was seventeen, so they got married the day after her seventeenth birthday.

I am the eldest of four: boy, boy, girl, boy. My youngest brother was born the day after my seventh birthday. There was actually another little girl between the second boy and girl, but she died shortly after birth due to being born three months premature. Nowadays, of course, she would have had a much better chance of survival. That's a lot of children in seven years, over nine-month clips, but that's the way it was for most dairy farm families of that time. You needed to get the "having kids" part of life quickly out of the way. The wives and the kids were needed for help on the farm. That might sound kind of harsh, but it's reality.

Dairy farmer wives of that day all had jobs. They bore the children, did most of the raising of the children in their early years, helped with the barn chores, helped with the field work, and got paid nothing—at least not money—but there was a lot of pride and love that came out of that "job," and there's not any amount of money that can replace that. The husbands just worked, worked, worked some more, and still found time to make babies. Enough said.

Growing up in the day and age of no color TV (we were lucky to have a TV that worked at all), no video games, no computers, no cell phones (just a party line telephone that was shared with some of the neighbors), you had to make your own fun. That wasn't hard to do living on the farm because there was always something to do. Activities were only limited by our imagination—and our imagination got us into trouble our fair share of the time, but usually nothing too serious.

Life was a pretty structured, regular thing: farm work and school on Monday through Friday, farm work on Saturdays, and church with minimal farm work on Sundays. Repeat, repeat . . . Dad would hire someone to milk the cows for a few days so we could take our yearly trip to Iowa to visit his parents. It was a real treat to have swimming lessons during the summer. Going to the Dairy Queen on Friday nights was a big treat too . . . my how times have changed. I remember going to my first Minnesota Twins game at the old Met Stadium. That was a huge treat. If it sounds like I didn't care for my childhood or thought it was too much work and not enough fun, it's actually the opposite. I absolutely loved it. I wouldn't have traded it for the world. Farming is good, hard work. I like working with my hands and enjoyed working with the animals. It's actually how I wanted to raise my family, but it didn't work out that way. More on that later.

Discipline wasn't a big deal. You knew where the "line" was, so you didn't cross it. I can honestly say that I can probably count on one hand the number of times Dad ever "took a hand" to me. A little "love tap" on the side of the "melon" was all that was needed. It was never a hard hit, just enough to get our attention, and it worked really well. If I got slapped, I deserved it. I remember one time I made Mom cry—don't remember what I did, but she was crying. It wasn't long after Dad got in the house that I was crying too. I made sure I never did that again. I think that a little "love tap" is fine when appropriate, as long as that's all it is.

Respect was a huge thing. I have always had the utmost respect for my parents. I was never afraid of them if I messed up. I was afraid of disappointing them, of letting them down. I knew I wasn't going to get beaten, I knew they were still going to love me. I just didn't want to see the look of disappointment on their faces. I've never looked up the definition of "respect," but part of it has got to be "not wanting to disappoint someone."

Mom and Dad raised us in a God-fearing home. It was two church services along with Sunday school every Sunday, and catechism after school on Wednesdays. Mom and Dad both taught Sunday school, Dad sat on the church board many times, and Mom sometimes sang in the choir. It was in Sunday school that Dad gave me the "sex talk." I must have been about fifteen or sixteen at the time and he was my Sunday school teacher (how much fun is that, having your parent as your Sunday school teacher?). The lesson that Sunday had to do with sex. Growing up on a farm with animals all over, you learned about the mechanics of sex at an early age. But Dad wasn't talking mechanics—he was talking about the who, when, and why of sex. He was trying to teach "there's a time and there's a place" for sex from the Bible's viewpoint. He looked—no, he *stared*—right at me while he was talking. It was almost as if there wasn't anyone in the room but the two of us. I don't know that I had been thinking about sex while sitting there in Sunday school, but if I had been, I wasn't anymore.

Mom and Dad got involved with church youth groups and even started a nondenominational group from the area communities. They were determined to give teenage kids something to do besides getting into trouble.

Every meal at home involved devotions and prayer, before and after eating. They went on many mission trips over the years to help others less fortunate. For more than twelve years until Mom's passing they went to a homeless shelter for men in St. Paul, Minnesota, on Tuesday and Thursday nights and helped serve supper. Dad still does that, and it's now been almost twenty years. As strong as their faith was, they were never pushy about it. If someone asked, they were more than willing to talk about it, but they didn't go around throwing it in your face. They lived it by example. Dad is that way to this day, even after all that has happened. I can't begin to tell you how much I respect that.

Mom and Dad were pretty passive people. By that I mean they didn't let things bother them too much. Things "bounced off" them pretty easily, especially Dad. I suppose that explains some of my passivity. There are plenty of times I should say something and don't. I like to avoid confrontation if I can, and Dad is the same way. I never once saw my parents argue (how many people can make that claim? My kids couldn't). Either they never argued or they made sure they did it when we kids weren't around. I remember my parents curling up on the couch together on Sunday afternoons for a nap. It was almost routine and I grew up thinking it was special and wanting that "routine" for myself someday. The love and respect they had for each other was something special. More on that later.

I think the most important thing Mom and Dad did was to always let us know how much we were loved. There were always plenty of hugs, kisses, and "I love yous" to go around. That didn't stop as we got older, not even as adults. I used to play a "game" with Mom where I would try to sneak out of the house without the usual hug and "love you." That was as recent as three and a half weeks before her passing away, and I never once made it out the door. I still can't get out of Dad's sight or off the phone without the same. That carried over with me raising my girls. I always told them I loved them, even after I yelled at them for something. My opinion: never discipline a child without telling him or her afterward that you love the child. That's why you're disciplining in the first place, because you love your children.

That, in a long nutshell, is me. It's not new news, but a lot of your personality comes from your childhood and how you were raised. Hopefully this gives you an idea of who I am. Why I am.

Somewhere In Between

L ife continued following that same basic routine for the next number of years. As time went on, we kids became involved in a few more activities such as 4-H. When I was in the seventh grade, Mom and Dad bought a "bigger and better" farm approximately nine miles west of the farm where we were living. It was kind of cool because it meant a larger and newer dairy barn, newer out-buildings, and a brand new house with a *bedroom of my own*. It also meant a different school district. I didn't think going to a new school was that big a deal. I already knew a few of the kids there and it didn't take long to get to know the rest. With approximately only seventy kids in my class, it wasn't that hard to get to know everyone. My brothers and sister adjusted well also.

When I was fourteen, my parents bought a grocery store in Baldwin. I'm not quiet sure what prompted that, but they did. Mom's brother had been helping on the farm some and had management experience, so he got the job of store manager. A store manager was needed because we still had the dairy farm to run. That meant there was always plenty to do. My brother Jerry and I would help at the store, mostly on Saturdays, by stocking shelves and carrying out groceries. Then it was back to the farm to milk the cows. Working in the grocery store was kind of fun. It was a nice change of pace working with customers instead of cows all the time. Of course every once in a while there was a customer who made you want to get back to the cows.

Like in most businesses, inventory had to be taken. It was a real pain having to count every last can and box on the shelves. Quite often it was done at night, after the customers were gone. One such night was Saturday, October 4, 1975. I was fifteen at the time. Dad had stayed in town to get the inventory finished while Mom took Jerry and me home.

After going through the normal routine of chores and milking, we had all the cows milked except one. For reasons too complicated and boring to explain, the one remaining cow to be milked was still outside. Jerry continued with some other chores while I went out to get her. It was dark in the pasture, so I took a flashlight with me. I also took a pitchfork along because the Holstein bull used for breeding the cows was also out there, and he had been acting kind of ornery for the last little bit. I still don't remember if I was chasing that last cow back to the barn or not, but I do know that I was headed toward the barn. I was only ten or fifteen feet from the end of the barn when I either heard or sensed something behind me. I turned around to see the bull ten feet away and charging at me with his head down. And he didn't look like he was in a playful mood . . .

Thank God I don't remember the beating. I do remember him catching up to me in about half a second, and I'm sure I didn't run more than two feet before he caught me. I remember his head hitting me in the back of my right thigh. I remember my feet leaving the ground, and then nothing . . .

Nothing until I woke up lying on my back in the dirt with the bull standing alongside me. When I say standing alongside me, I mean *standing alongside me*. There was no way you could have gotten a hair between his front hooves and my right side. He occasionally stomped on the ground, and when he did I felt his hooves rubbing against my ribs. He never had his face far from mine or from the upper half of my body. All the while he was breathing directly on me. His hot breath against me smelled awful. Actually, it downright stank. And there was phlegm dripping from his nose and landing on me, sometimes on my face, sometimes on my chest and stomach. He wasn't being extremely noisy, but he wasn't quiet, either. Most people have heard a cow or bull "moo." Forget that sound; he didn't sound anything like that. He had the deepest, most terrifying, evil-sounding bellow you could possibly imagine. It was the sound of a wild animal that had "tasted blood" and wanted more. I can still hear him . . .

I knew I was injured. I just didn't know how bad. My chest hurt terribly and my stomach didn't feel much better. Then there was my jaw, which was pretty much lying on my chest. There was no doubt in my mind that it was broken . . . badly. My tongue felt thick, but I could still feel teeth scattered all through the bottom of my mouth.

I knew enough not to move or try to get away. There was an electric fence not that far away, but I figured that even if I could get to it to crawl under it, he would go right through it anyway. When I'd move my legs a little (partly to see if they still worked), he would give me a nudge in the ribs. It didn't feel good when he did that. I knew I was pretty much planted there until someone came looking for me.

From where I was lying I couldn't see the pitchfork, but I could see the flashlight, which was still on. That's what Jerry saw first, the flashlight. He had continued on with some other chores (some of which were in other buildings), and after approximately thirty minutes realized I wasn't around and that the last cow still hadn't been milked.

After searching the barn and not finding me, he headed out to the pasture. That's when he saw the flashlight. He didn't yet see me and was calling my name as he walked. Then he saw me and the bull "protecting" me. I don't know what he was thinking, but he kept walking closer. I'm sure he was in total disbelief about what he was seeing, besides wanting to do something to help his brother. He kept calling my name as he got closer. I tried telling him to get away, but it wasn't easy to talk with my jaw hanging the way it was. Try it once—try talking with your mouth hanging open and not moving your lower jaw very much.

He couldn't hear me, couldn't understand me, or just didn't care because he kept getting closer. That's when it happened. The bull had had enough. He charged Jerry and knocked him down too.

Fortunately for Jerry the bull was satisfied with whom he already had. He came right back to me and stood guard again. Jerry wasn't injured and headed for the house just as fast as he could.

Like I said, Dad was in town working at the grocery store while all of this took place. Mom would later tell me how much that bothered Dad for a long time, the fact that he wasn't home when it happened. She said he lost a lot of sleep over it, that he blamed himself. I never felt that way; it would have happened whether he was there or not. Thirty years later I would end up understanding all too well exactly how he felt.

Visiting with Mom in the house at the time of the attack was a guy named Mark. Mark was one of the young adults who attended the nondenominational youth group Mom and Dad had started. He must have been around twenty at the time.

Jerry ran in the house and told them what had happened. The three of them found Dad's shotgun but couldn't find any bullets. Dad had done a good job of keeping them in separate places. It's just as well they didn't find the bullets. What if they had missed the target and only wounded the bull? It was dark out there and it would have been hard to get a good shot at him. He was already crabby, and I certainly wouldn't have wanted him any madder. And what if they did get a good shot at him? Because he was standing as close as he was to me, guess where he was going to land? I was already hurting. I didn't need that too. Then there's always the chance they would have shot me . . . but they didn't find the bullets, so none of it happened.

While Mark and Jerry headed for the barn and pasture, Mom tried to call Dad. Either he was busy in the store and didn't hear the phone or Mom dialed wrong from being shook up. I'm not sure at what point Dad found out what was going on, but he didn't see me until he reached the Baldwin Hospital.

On their way to the barn, Jerry and Mark flagged down a passing car. In the car was our neighbor, Al, and his girlfriend. Al must have been about the same age as Mark. I don't know that you want to call it a miracle, but it was a fortunate thing to have someone happen to be driving by at that particular time. Ours were country roads with only a house or two every mile. You might go all day and not see anyone drive by. At any rate, Al was there now and was ready to help.

Jerry, Mark, and Al headed for the barn. Mom, Al's girlfriend, my sister, Jody, and my youngest brother Joe stood outside the pasture gate looking toward me.

When the three guys got close to me, they started yelling and screaming at the bull, trying to scare him away. He didn't budge. They then grabbed some rocks, pieces of wood, and anything else they could find. They threw enough stuff and yelled and screamed enough so he backed off far enough so one of the older guys could drag me into the barn. They quickly closed the heavy steel gate securing the doorway to the barn. *I was safe.* The bull went absolutely nuts. He ran wild with that terrible, evil bellowing.

I walked to the house. I don't actually remember much of it, but I walked. Our house was a split level and I sat on the stairs in the foyer leading up while they tried to decide what to do with me. This was 1975, and there was no such thing as 911. You had to look in the phone book for the phone number for an ambulance. Mom had gone to the house a little before I got there to try to figure out what to do, who to call. There were all different numbers for fire, police, and ambulance. All towns had police, but only some had fire and/or ambulance. There were towns that were closer to us, but the closest one with an ambulance was ten miles away. To make matters worse, our driveway was the dividing line for fire/ambulance/telephone services. We actually had a phone in the house with lines from two different exchanges coming into it because neither phone company wanted to give up the rights to the area.

When you finally figured out which emergency number to call, the phone didn't ring in a dispatch center, it rang at someone's house. After a number of attempts to get hold of someone and not being confident they knew where we were, it was decided that Al would drive us to the hospital in Baldwin. Mom, Al, his girlfriend, and I headed for the hospital. I don't remember any of the ride, but Al said that he hit a hundred mph more than once on the way there.

We found out later that an ambulance had headed toward the farm from a town ten miles or so, the opposite direction of Baldwin. I don't recall the reasoning they didn't get all the way to the farm, but we had left by that time anyway.

I don't remember more than just a few moments at the Baldwin Hospital. I remember standing outside the hospital waiting for someone to come to the emergency room door after the "night button" had been rung. I remember the "oh shit" look on the nurse's face when she opened the door and saw me. I remember sitting in the wheelchair waiting for the elevator doors to open, and that's the end of it, nothing more. I don't even remember Dad getting there.

My left lung collapsed when they laid me down on the table in the emergency room. They said that was good timing because I would have had a hard time walking to the house and so forth if it had collapsed sooner. They got me out of my "barn clothes" and somewhat cleaned up. I had been covered in blood, dirt, and of course, cow manure.

The doctor in Baldwin decided to send me to St. Joseph's Hospital in St. Paul, Minnesota. St. Joseph's is a Catholic-based hospital. We weren't Catholic, but the Baldwin doctor knew a doctor who worked at the St. Paul hospital who was good at putting faces back together. The Baldwin Hospital didn't have the same problems we did getting hold of an ambulance; of course it was there and ready to go. I don't remember even one second of the ride to St. Joseph's.

Mom and Dad rode with us, along with a nurse and the driver. I don't know if anyone else was there. They said they set a new speed record getting to St. Paul. That speed record only lasted two or three weeks. A kid who was a year younger than me and went to the same school I did was severely burned in a farm accident. He spent six weeks in the hospital.

The next thing I remember is lying on the bed in the emergency room of St. Joseph's. I had a tremendous amount of pain in my face, chest, and abdomen. Breathing wasn't an easy thing to do with a collapsed lung.

At this point, things started getting a little "weird." I remember it so vividly, like it's happening right now. I still get goose bumps just thinking about it. I heard the voices of people in the emergency room: the doctors, nurses, Mom, and Dad. There was noise besides that of voices, such as medical instruments and machines. I remember faces: the doctor's, the nurse's, Mom's, Dad's—and mine. That's right, *mine*. I could clearly see mine because I was no longer hearing or seeing *anything* from the *bed* of that emergency room. *Everything* I heard and saw came from the vantage point of the *ceiling* of that emergency room!

I was "floating" by the ceiling looking down at everyone and everything in that emergency room. I know about when I got there but really have no idea how I got there. I don't remember a feeling of "leaving" my body; it was just a matter of being on the bed one second and up by the ceiling the next. Even though I was only fifteen and hadn't experienced many things in my lifetime, I knew what I was experiencing was far from normal.

As I looked down, I could see Mom and Dad crying and looking very stressed, and I wasn't looking very good either. I now understood the "oh shit" look on the nurse's face back in Baldwin. My jaw was a mess. It was hanging open, halfway lying on my chest. I could see the teeth scattered around in my mouth. My lower lip was hanging down because there was a big cut, half an inch or so below my mouth, that was almost the width of my mouth. My face was beginning to swell from the beating it had taken. It hurt like crazy to breath . . . it just plain hurt . . . terrible . . . everywhere. I was trying to figure out how I could hurt so bad when I wasn't even in my body.

I was having a hard time understanding what was going on. I knew I wasn't dead because I could see that my arms were still moving, that I would hold Mom and Dad's hands, and I was breathing. Every once in a while I would try to say something to Mom or Dad, to answer a doctor's question. I was thinking this "out-of-body" thing only happens when you were dead, or at least unconscious. That's when it hit me: I wasn't dead, but I was about to be. I was the process of making the transition from life to death. I was somewhere in between.

From my perch by the ceiling I could see a crucifix on the wall on the other end of the room. Not being Catholic, I don't know that I even knew what a crucifix was, but just the same, I saw a cross and was thinking being by it might be a good idea. And I decided that if I was going to be "checking out" for good, I might as well get a "head start" getting closer to God. So I "floated" over to it and couldn't believe what happened. The pain was gone! I don't just mean better, I mean *gone*! It was the most peaceful, relaxing, everything-good feeling you could ever imagine. Take the best feeling you've ever had in your life and multiply it by a thousand, and that's where I was. I didn't see God and there wasn't a bright light at the end of a tunnel like some people have seen, but I was pretty happy with where I was at. Except . . .

From the crucifix I couldn't see Mom and Dad or hear what the doctors were saying. So I floated back over to my body. Grandpa was there now comforting Mom and Dad. I wasn't looking any better, that's for sure. As I got closer, the pain returned with a vengeance. I heard the doctors telling Mom and Dad that my spleen would be coming out, that they weren't sure what other internal damage there was. That they could tell from the X-rays that the bull had stood on my chest and then used his head to smash my jaw to pieces. That there would be two surgeons working on me at the same time, one on my face, the other on the internal stuff. That I had youth on my side. That they would do everything they could, but no guarantees that I would make it out of surgery. That last part wasn't something I wanted to hear. I had heard enough, so back to the crucifix I went. Just like that, the pain was gone again.

I sure liked not having the pain, but it bothered me not being able to see Mom and Dad, so back to them I went. They were heartbroken. The only time I had ever seen Dad cry before was when his dad had died, and it was hard to watch. It was so bizarre watching myself try to talk to them. The whole situation was bizarre. I still couldn't understand how I could be in two places at the same time.

The doctors were done talking and had left the room. At least that part was good, no talking doctors meant no more "bad news." But the pain was unbearable, so back to the crucifix I went. That was my last "trip." Shortly after that, they came in with a different bed to take me to the operating room. Mom and Dad walked alongside me as we were leaving the emergency room.

As they were taking me away, I took a long, hard look at Mom, Dad and my body. I figured just in case . . . one last look . . . goodbye to Mom and Dad . . . goodbye to myself . . .

You can't even imagine the feeling . . .

The surgery lasted a little better than four hours, making it a good decision, at least in my mind, to be operating on both places at the same time. My jaw was broke in two places, once on each side. The right side was broke toward the back of my mouth where the bone gets really tall. The doctors said it took a lot of force for the bone to break there. The left side was broken toward the front. A piece of jawbone along with two teeth were missing there. They made an incision under my chin at that break and used wire to tie the bone ends together. Fake teeth were added several months later. My mouth was wired shut for seven and a half weeks. As time went on, the spot where the two teeth were missing came in handy for getting a straw into my mouth. I lived on strawberry malts and tomato soup for the time my mouth was wired shut after leaving the hospital.

Two things proved interesting while having my mouth wired shut: yawning and sneezing. Everyone yawns every day, probably with not much thought given to it. But try it once with your teeth clenched together; not so easily done. Sneezing was even worse. I have always been a hard sneezer, the kind of sneeze the neighbors can hear. I had a couple of times while my mouth was wired that I sneezed so hard I thought brain matter was going to come out of my ears. It hurt, really hurt. My ears actually plugged up a couple of times after sneezes. I think they were just vapor-locked, not brain-matter plugged.

I'd had a tracheotomy. That's an incision made in the throat with a tube placed in it. With all the swelling that was in my face and a tube going in my nose, I needed a way to get air. Also because the left lung was collapsed, a machine was hooked up to the trach tube that forced moisture into my throat. That moisture was used to help break up the mucous that was coming out of my lung as it inflated.

I had four broken ribs on each side of my chest. On my chest X-rays, they could see part of the bull's hoof print on my sternum. Like I said before, they could tell he had stood on my chest and then used his head to break my jaw. I guess that would easily explain some of the pain I felt in my chest. When the bull was shipped to the market the next day, he weighed in at 1,847 pounds. I'm sure glad they only saw *one* hoof print on the X-rays. I'm also glad bulls used on dairy farms are dehorned when they are young. Can you imagine what would have happened if he'd had horns like the bulls used in bull fights? I would have ended up being nothing more than a hood ornament for the bull.

I had a six-inch vertical incision on my belly. They did the internal repairs from there and fixed a tear in my diaphragm. They also removed my appendix while they were "in the area." I thought that was kind of cool, one less thing to go wrong another day.

I did a lot of coughing the first week and a half as a result of the lung inflating and mucous coming up. That hurt terribly of course, considering the broken ribs and the belly incision. I kept a pillow close by to hold against myself whenever I coughed; it seemed to help some. Morphine was my friend. I got a shot in my rear end every four hours around the clock for a week straight. I was usually asking for another one before the four-hour mark was up.

The tube that went up my nose ended in my stomach and was first used to keep my stomach empty. After four days the process was reversed and it was then used to feed me. My stomach wasn't so crazy about the feeding direction at first. Sometime during the night they "switched directions" of the tube, and I felt myself get sick. I hit the buzzer and two nurses appeared lickity split. I started to vomit, and it was coming out of the trach tube. Obviously it couldn't come out of my mouth; it was wired shut. The nurses quickly inflated a bag around the trach tube. Otherwise the vomit would have gone back down into my lungs and I would have drowned. The trach tube was removed before I left the hospital, so they sent pocket scissors home with me so I could remove the bands holding my mouth shut if I got sick again. They said that was a close call and didn't want it to happen again. I didn't want it happening again either.

I spent one week in ICU and another five days after that at St. Joseph's. A day or so after the feeding tube incident, I made Mom cry again. It happened when she first walked into my ICU room that morning. Like I said before, part of the function of a trach tube is to help you get air when the normal way isn't available. Because there is a big hole in the end of the tube where the air enters and exits, you can't talk without covering the hole. You have to cover it, or there's no air getting to your voice box to make it work. This was, for a number of reasons, the first time I was able to put my finger over the hole. Also, I wasn't well enough to talk prior to this. I had been using a pen and paper to communicate.

When Mom walked into the room, I covered the hole and simply said, "Hi, Mom." I can still see the look on her face and the tears running down her cheeks. She said that meant more to her than the first time I ever said "Mom" as a toddler. Thirty-four years later I would understand exactly how she felt. As she said, "Sometimes the *second* first time is way more special than the *first* first time."

Physically I was left with a number of scars. I have a scar from the cut under my lower lip and one under my chin from the surgery to repair my jaw. The scars on my throat, chest, and stomach are now covered with body hair. The only scar anyone sees or that bothers me is the one under my lip. It's right out there for everyone to see. But it's been there for more than thirty-five years and most people don't know me any other way. I consider it a "battle scar," a battle I figure to be in the "win" column for me because the bull was dead the next day and I wasn't.

As a result of my jaw being broken on the left side, along with part of the bone missing, there was some nerve damage because the nerve runs through the jawbone there. That caused a reduced amount of sensation in the chin area. Because of the reduced sensation there, I tend to sometimes nick myself while shaving, especially when using a new razor blade. Also, I occasionally end up with food hanging off my chin. Usually someone I know will tell me about it before I end up walking around that way for too long. And that first winter and summer I could tell you every time it was going to snow or rain because my jaw would hurt like crazy. I haven't had any troubles with anything since.

Emotionally, I really don't have any "scars," at least not what I would call scars. I have never even once had a dream of any kind about the bull attack. You'd think I would have had all kinds of nightmares about it. In fact, I wasn't even left with a fear of bulls. I even went as far as having some around when I started milking cows again after school. While I wasn't afraid of them, I did keep an eye on them and showed them plenty of respect.

October 4, the anniversary of the attack, ended up being just as much or more of a "birthday" to me than my real birthday in February. Mom would even make a birthday cake for me on that day. I always saw it as the day my life started over, the day I was given a second chance. My biological birthday was just the day marking the anniversary of my body getting another year older. My "bull birthday" marks the anniversary of the day that my "spirit" was given new life. My spirit may get tired from time to time, but it will *never* grow old.

As you can imagine, my time spent "somewhere in between" was unnerving, to say the least. I still have a hard time understanding how I was able to "be in two places at the same time." How could my "body" be on the bed while moving and trying to talk at the same time "I" was by the ceiling "seeing" and "thinking"? I guess it ultimately doesn't matter how or why it happened, but it's something I will wonder about until the day I die—for real.

I know I was never clinically dead like some people are when they have an experience; I was alive the whole time. Maybe it's better that I was alive when it happened. That way I know it was real. I know it wasn't something that was dreamed up because I was unconscious or drugged up. At that point I hadn't even been given any painkillers yet. That doesn't mean I don't believe people who say they had an experience when they were dead, even if they'd received drugs. I most definitely believe them, and love listening to their stories about what happened to them and "where" they were. I'm just glad that for me, it happened the way it did. When it comes right down to it, I don't know just "where" I was, and I don't think it much matters. It happened, and it's as clear to me as if it was happening right now.

That event has affected my life in a number of ways. For starters, I look at some things differently now and I am the eternal optimist. Some who know me would say too much so. They're probably right, but after living through that, it's hard *not* to think that everything is going to be okay. I know that sounds weird after all that has happened since then, but it's how I feel.

Much like my dad, I was always a laid-back person, but I think this experience added to that. It's hard for me to get really upset. Trust me, it can be done. I can get all whipped up, but I usually let things go pretty quickly and move on. As we all know, life's too short to be holding things inside. In most cases, it could be worse than what it is . . . whatever "it" is.

As I said before, I was raised in a God-fearing home and have always had a belief or faith in God. My understanding of the word "faith" is believing or trusting in someone or something. Sometimes, as in the case of God, that believing is in someone, or something you can't see or touch. I suppose maybe some of my faith comes from going to church and Sunday school regularly. I know some of my faith comes from watching Mom and Dad. As I said before, they very much displayed their faith and beliefs by the way they lived their lives and the examples they set.

I know a *large* part of my faith comes from the "ceiling" of that hospital emergency room. There is *no one* who will ever convince me there isn't a God. While I didn't see God, I know he's there. It would be hard to imagine anyone else live through the same experience and not feel the same way. I don't know just who or what God is, and there are things I don't understand, like how God has no beginning or end, or that he's always been there and always will be. I don't understand how that is possible. But I guess I don't need to understand. *Faith.* I know God is there. And I know there is something after this life, something bigger and better. If I could feel the *great* feeling I had just being by a crucifix on a wall, imagine how good Mom and Stormi feel being in the real place, heaven itself!

Ever since that experience, I have wondered: At what point does our "soul," "spirit," or whatever it is that is within us leave? Is that what was happening to me? My soul was leaving? And why did it happen to me? There certainly have been plenty of other people who were injured much worse than I was and didn't have an "experience." Was I being prepared for what was going to happen thirty years later?

This part is hard to explain. Since becoming an EMT in 2002, I have performed CPR on a number of people. I have not had an opportunity to talk to anyone afterward who survived whatever injury or illness got them to the point of CPR. But I do find myself wondering "where" the person receiving CPR is. Is he or she still in his or her body? Is the person floating around the room like I was? If the person does end up dying, how soon does he or she leave and move on to the next level? This may sound strange, but if the patient dies, I have found myself "looking around" the room wondering if the person's still there or if he or she has already left. I wish I could, but obviously I can't ask someone who ended up making a complete final journey what happened, what the person saw . . . or didn't see.

As you can probably tell, the "somewhere in between" experience left me with a number of questions. It may even seem like I have more questions than answers, and maybe so. But at least in my mind, the answers and comfort I received while spending time "somewhere in between" far outweigh any remaining questions I have. I can't think of any knowledge I have gained in life that's as valuable to me as the knowledge I gained while near death.

While I can't say I was crazy about all the pain I went through and am not looking to take on another bull, I am extremely grateful for the experience I had. It has helped dry many a tear since 2005 because I know Mom and Stormi are okay. I can't imagine going through losing them without having had my own experience first. The experience made what was to come thirty years down the road much easier to handle.

*   *   *

Neighbors and uncles helped finish the chores the night of the attack and took care of everything the following day or two until Dad felt comfortable leaving the hospital. After the attack, the bull continued being very "vocal" and "restless" until the truck showed up the next day to take him to market. Those who helped load him into the truck knew better than to walk into the yard/pasture unprotected. They entered the yard driving a tractor to herd him toward the truck. The bull was still not in a cooperative mood. He placed his head on the manure bucket on the front of the tractor and pushed the tractor in a circle before relenting and getting on the truck. I guess it shows just how strong he was. I'm glad my jaw was broken in only two places.

*   *   *

The bull attacked me on a Saturday night, and on the following Monday, Jerry broke his arm at school while in gym class. As Mom and Dad said, "When it rains, it pours." As soon as I was able, I teased him that he broke it on purpose because he was looking for some attention too. Broken arm or not, I still convinced him to make strawberry malts for me when I got out of the hospital. I think they call it "brotherly love."

*   *   *

Mark died in 1994 at age forty from leukemia. Talk about completely helpless feelings. Mark had risked his own life to help save mine, and then when the time came that his life was in danger, I wasn't able to do anything to help save it. There is something that is very unfair and wrong with that. I will never forget you and what you did for me, Mark. Thank you and God bless.

Death of Ma Sue

It was Sunday afternoon, September 11, 2005. I was working at an open house for a model home when my cell phone rang. It was Dad calling. For years he and Mom had called each of us four kids on Sundays to say hi. My sister, me, and our families have always lived in the same area as Mom and Dad, but my brothers and their families have always lived out of state. The call was Mom and Dad's way of catching up on the news of the week from each of us, especially with my brothers, whom they didn't get to see as often. I assumed that was the purpose of his call, but I couldn't have been more wrong.

I could hear the concern in his voice as soon as I answered. He was calling to tell me that Mom, Ma Sue as all the grandchildren called her, was developing some complications from her knee surgery three days earlier. At least it was thought to be complications from the surgery. I thought right away he was going to say that she needed another blood transfusion, because she had received a transfusion the day after the surgery due to her hemoglobin being low. Again, I wasn't even close.

Dad said Ma Sue was having difficulty breathing. I sure didn't see that one coming. I asked if she was being given oxygen and he said he wasn't sure. He did know she was going to be transferred from the Baldwin Hospital to United Hospital in St. Paul. I knew that United is a hospital well-known for people with pulmonary issues. That concerned me somewhat. I couldn't understand why someone who had knee surgery would be having a hard time breathing. Dad said an ambulance would be arriving shortly to transport her to United. I asked if he wanted me to find a replacement for myself at the open house and head for St. Paul, but he said that wasn't necessary and that I should finish out my shift. I told him I would see him later and to please give Ma Sue my love.

Not even half an hour later my phone rang again, and once again it was Dad. I was thinking as I answered that he must be calling to let me know he was on his way to United. For the third time in fewer then thirty minutes, I was way off with my assumptions. This time there was more then concern in Dad's voice. There was the crackling of emotion as he spoke. He was calling to tell me that the plans had changed, that Ma Sue's condition had worsened, and a helicopter was en route to get her to United as quickly as possible. This time I didn't bother asking Dad if I should head for the hospital. I found a replacement for myself at the model home and headed for United. I called my girls on my way and filled them in with what was going on.

Little did I know this would be my first of many trips to United over the next several weeks. Little did I know this would end up being a one-way trip for Ma Sue.

Ma Sue

Suzanna Hendrena Zevenbergen was born October 16, 1941, in Orange City, Iowa. I remember Grandpa Zevenbergen telling the story of what happened the day Mom was baptized. When they got home from church, they heard on the radio that Pearl Harbor had been bombed. Like me, Mom was the oldest of six children in her family. As is the case for a lot of those who are the oldest child, Mom was a great help to Grandma with taking care of her younger siblings.

Mom's parents moved the family to a dairy farm north of Baldwin, Wisconsin, in 1956. As was quite common for that day and age, Mom only went to school as far as the eighth grade, and then it was off to work. Years later she went back to school to get her GED. Mom was understandably proud of that achievement and we had a graduation party for her.

After her family moved to Wisconsin, Mom worked as a cashier in a grocery store and also worked for a business that supplied eggs to grocery stores. Mom's job there was to "candle" eggs. That was the method for checking eggs for quality and to make sure they weren't fertilized. The eggs were all held up to a light one at a time. The light was bright enough that you could see through the eggshell and see the contents, thereby being able to confirm its quality.

Dad spent two years in the army serving in Korea. Upon returning home from Korea in 1956, Dad went to college for one year. In 1957 he moved to Wisconsin and bought a farm approximately four miles from Grandpa and Grandma's farm. Grandma Zevenbergen would occasionally bring Dad some home cooking so he didn't go hungry because of his limited cooking skills. Dad lived on the farm by himself until they got married in 1958. I was born eighteen months after Mom and Dad married, and Dad's "work force" was off and running.

I spent some of my time growing up in the dairy barn. Mom took care of the household duties but was also a huge help to Dad out in the barn and in the fields. There wasn't much else Mom could do but take me out to the barn with her when she was out there helping with chores. That changed somewhat as my siblings were born because Mom couldn't keep an eye on everyone plus work.

Mom was always a hard worker. When we moved to a larger farm, she was right there with Dad helping with the increased workload. When they bought the grocery store, Mom was right there working alongside Dad, working again as a cashier, and working at home. When Dad got involved in home construction and real estate, once again Mom was right there working side-by-side with Dad in the office and taking care of floor covering sales. As the years went on and Mom started to develop arthritis, it became harder and harder to keep up with the same workload, but Mom did her best and seldom complained.

I remember the thrill in Mom's voice when she was told she was going to be a grandma. It was something she had talked about for some time, occasionally dropping hints that she wasn't getting any younger and that she was "ready." Mom lived for her grandchildren and spoiled them rotten every chance she got. She was proud to be known as Ma Sue. It was a name all her own, meant just for her. Ma Sue cherished her grandchildren. I know she would have been terribly heartbroken if her granddaughter Stormi had died before she did.

Over the years, Ma Sue had a number of joints repaired or replaced due to her arthritis. She had had the first knee replaced in 2004, and everything had gone smoothly. When Ma Sue and Dad planned their mission trip to Africa, she decided she wanted the second knee replaced and healed up before they left so she would be able to be more active while there.

The trip to Africa was to start on the fourth of November, and Ma Sue had the surgery done on September 8. I happened to be at the hospital for an appointment of my own that day. I'd had a bit of a "blood scare." Actually, it was a pretty good scare. They thought at one point it might even be leukemia. Thankfully it turned out to be something much less severe and easier to treat.

I walked out of the room where my doctor's appointment was and arrived at Ma Sue's room as they brought her in from surgery. I stayed to talk to her, but Ma Sue was still groggy so I didn't stay long. Because of my work schedule, I didn't get to the hospital on Friday or Saturday.

The next time I saw Ma Sue she was in an ICU unit with an oxygen mask covering her face.

Ma Sue had been placed in an ICU unit upon arrival at United Hospital. It wasn't immediately known what was wrong with her other than she was having breathing difficulties thought to be related to her knee surgery. Multiple tests were run to try to find the source of the problem. She had received a blood transfusion on Saturday because her hemoglobin was low, but it was unknown if that had anything to do with the problems she was now having. It was known that she hadn't aspirated (vomited) during surgery. If that happens, fluid can get into a patient's lungs and cause breathing difficulties or even pneumonia.

For the first few days Ma Sue was at United, it was a matter of trying to figure out was wrong, what had injured her lungs, as well as making sure her breathing didn't get any worse. She was continuously on oxygen and they tried different saturation levels to find what worked best. Her heart was ruled out as the source of any of her breathing problems. They took multiple X-rays each day to monitor any changes.

It was decided on Friday, September 16 to place Ma Sue on a ventilator. The doctors felt it would be best if Ma Sue was placed on a ventilator for two reasons. First, the ventilator would do a much better job of getting good oxygen flow to her injured lungs than what just an oxygen mask was doing. Second, they would have better access to her lungs via the tubing to take samples.

Ma Sue was understandably upset about being put on a ventilator. She was concerned that once she was on it, they wouldn't be able to remove it. She was assured by the doctors it was only temporary and that as soon as whatever had injured her lungs was resolved, the ventilator would be removed. There were a couple of times while I was an EMT that I wished I hadn't been one because people would occasionally ask me questions I wasn't qualified to answer. This was one of those times because Ma Sue asked me what I thought about being placed on a ventilator. I didn't know what to say other then to reiterate what the doctors had said, so I told her it was the right thing to do, reassuring her again that the ventilator was only temporary. It was the last time I ever talked to Ma Sue without a tube in her mouth that went down into her lungs. For the first few days she was able to talk some, but after that she was sedated and unable to talk at all. I grew to hate that tube, a hatred that intensified by leaps and bounds over the next four years.

Also on Friday, my sister, Jody, put an entry on the Caring Bridge website for the first time regarding Ma Sue. Jody had heard of Caring Bridge before, but I hadn't. What a wonderful website Caring Bridge is. It allows families to post updates about their loved one online as often as they want. That way, all anyone who wants to check on the status of a sick or injured friend or loved one has to do is log on to Caring Bridge. They will then know that the information they are reading is up to date and accurate, instead of hearing it secondhand from someone else.

Jody had waited start a site for Ma Sue because we thought she was only going to be hospitalized for a few days. Jody did all the journal updates, but I signed in on the site's guestbook a few times. One of the things I wrote about was the devotion between Mom and Dad. As I wrote at that time, it was "something fairy tales were made of." I had never seen Ma Sue and Dad argue. I had never seen them do anything but show the utmost love and respect for each other. I had never seen them not set a good loving example for us kids or for their grandchildren. They enjoyed being around each other and it showed. It truly was something fairy tales were made of.

We tried to get Dad to go home to get some decent sleep in his own bed, but he wouldn't leave. He chose to spend most nights in a recliner in Ma Sue's room. One of us kids stayed each night as well.

There were days Ma Sue made some progress, but there were more bad days than good days. It seemed like for every step forward there were two steps going backward. They just couldn't get a handle on what was making Ma Sue's lungs not work properly. A biopsy was scheduled to be taken of her lungs but had to be cancelled because she wasn't healthy enough for it.

On September 20, Ma Sue was placed in a newly developed bed called a "rotoprone bed." It's a bed in which the patient is lying prone, or facedown. The bed can also swing side to side at different angles. The swinging from side to side can be done manually or automatically. The thought process behind the bed is that studies had shown that patients with injured lungs had better healing results while lying prone. There was an incredible amount of padding involved with the bed so Ma Sue didn't get bed sores from pressure points caused by the straps while basically hanging there. Once Ma Sue was fully positioned in her rotoprone bed, about the only thing you could see was her face. Also, by this time Ma Sue was heavily sedated.

The rotoprone bed helped at first, but then the forward progress seemed to stop again. Around the same time, we heard the news that we never wanted to hear. The reason for Ma Sue's breathing problems, the reason her lungs were injured was because she had developed Adult Respiratory Distress Syndrome (ARDS). They told us ARDS can be caused by one of four things: aspiration during surgery, infection, blood transfusion, or unknown reasons. Since no one reason could be determined for sure, Ma Sue fell into the category of "unknown." They also told us that there is at best a 50 percent survival rate for patients with ARDS. They told us that the older the patient is, the less likely the chance of survival.

Ma Sue fought very hard, and she fought for a long time, but on October 3, she went "home" to heaven. They had told us the day before that her organs were starting to shut down, so most of her family had a chance to say goodbye before she took her last breath. The four of us kids sat with her and told stories of when we were growing up; we laughed until we cried, and we cried until we laughed. I will never forget the look of utter devastation on Dad's face. Their fairy tale had come to an end. I will never forget having to take my grandpa, Ma Sue's dad, by the hand and walk him to her room, telling him that my mom, his little girl, was dying. Up to that point in my life, it was the longest walk of my life. Had I only known how many times those scenes were going to be replayed over the next four years. I know it's going to sound strange, but as Ma Sue was taking her final breaths, I "looked" around the room for her. I couldn't help but wonder if she was "floating," and watching over us on her way to heaven. Sometimes I have even wondered if she was "floating" for a long period of time like I was and was crying with us during her final earthly moments.

The O'Connell Funeral Home "family" did a wonderful job of helping us with the arrangements for Ma Sue's visitation and funeral. Ma Sue had collected porcelain dolls and Precious Moments figurines for years and the funeral was decorated with some of them for her visitation. Her funeral was a beautiful testament to her life. At the cemetery during her committal, my siblings and I each got to release a dove into the air. We were heartbroken that our beloved Ma Sue was gone, but we took comfort in knowing she was in a better place and wasn't suffering anymore.

I remember Mom being a loving person who always put others, especially her family, ahead of herself. I remember Mom as a loving and devoted wife. I remember Mom as a person who didn't just say, "I love you," she showed it by her actions. I remember Mom as being a person who was always very patient with us kids and later on with her grandchildren. I remember Mom as being a God-fearing woman who made sure us kids knew who God is. I remember Mom as being the *best* mom.

I will close this by repeating what I said at the end of Mom's eulogy:

"I could not have asked for a better mother. I love you and will miss you terribly."

Love,
Jeff

Death: Stormi Liz

I'm normally out of bed by 7:00 in the morning, but it was a Saturday and I hadn't slept that great the night before. I was lying there thinking about getting my lazy butt up when my ambulance pager went off a little before 7:10. I wasn't "on call," and besides that, the address given for a one-car rollover was about two miles west of where my ambulance's service area ended. In other words, I didn't get up and make a beeline for the ambulance garage.

But as I lay there in bed, I had this sick feeling that it was my daughter, Stormi, who was in the accident. No . . . it wasn't just a sick feeling . . . I knew it was Stormi. I just knew. It was one of those times when a feeling comes over you and you instantly get sick to your stomach. I knew partly because of the information given on the page: the page was for a one-car roll over with *female* occupant ejected from the *car* and found lying unconscious on the ground with arms moving. Also, the *address* given was in an area where friends of hers lived. I think the rest was just plain parental instinct. I'm still not exactly sure why I didn't get up and go anyway. Maybe partly because one big fear of being an EMT is going on a run and finding out that it involves family or friends. Maybe it was because I didn't want to believe it could be true.

Whatever the reason, after fewer than ten minutes of lying there trying to decide what to do, the doorbell rang. A lot of doubt that it could be Stormi was now gone from my mind. It was too much of a coincidence to have the pager go off and the doorbell ringing that close together. I quickly pulled on a pair of jeans and ran down the stairs toward the front door. By the time I got to the bottom of the stairs, the ringing of the doorbell had changed to a pounding on the door. More hope/doubt gone. As I got to the door I could see the person there was Sandy, my ambulance director. Rest of the hope/doubt gone.

I opened the door, and before she could say a word, I said, "It's Stormi, isn't it?"

She replied, "Yes, we've got to go."

I yelled up the stairs to the rest of the family that it had been Stormi that was in the accident announced on the pager and that I was headed for the hospital.

It was a cold November morning and Sandy's car's windshield was all frosted up. Sandy had received a call from the Baldwin ambulance director who was at the scene of the accident, and she hadn't taken the time to scrape her windshield before leaving her home. She had driven to my house with her head hanging out her car window.

My car was garaged, so the windshield was clear. I drove, and she tried to keep me calm. Let's just say that I didn't drive fifty-five. I asked her how bad it was, and she said she didn't know.

When we got to the Baldwin Hospital, I pulled up and parked in front of the main entrance like I owned the place. Because of my volunteering as an EMT, I knew my way around the hospital and headed right for the emergency room. There was no way I was prepared for what I was about to see. They were doing CPR on my daughter, my baby, my Stormi Liz.

The shock of it stopped me dead in my tracks. The room started to spin.

Stormi Elizabeth Hielkema

S tormi was almost two days old before her name was set in stone. The nurses at the hospital were actually starting to get on her mother and me to decide for sure what her name was going to be. It's funny, but now I can't even tell you what other name ideas we had for a girl, or if we even had any. Her mother had found the name Stormi in a baby name book. I had never heard the name before and wasn't sure it was a name I wanted for our child. I didn't want to name her something that she was going to be picked on for. A great-aunt would later say that it sounded like a name for a horse. Finally, my mom said it was a beautiful name and we shouldn't worry about what other people thought. I guess that was all we needed to hear because that's when it got decided for sure. As the years went on I can only remember a handful of times anyone said anything about her name. The great-aunt is the only one I ever recall saying anything negative. Most thought it was a unique name, just like Stormi was a unique person. As far as I know, no kids in school ever teased her about her name.

One thing I find interesting as I write this: thank God for spell-check, but every time I type the name Stormi, it gets a red line under it telling me I have spelled it wrong. I guess the name is unique. It's not even in spell-check, at least not spelled the way hers was.

Her middle name, Elizabeth, was in honor of my mom's mom, Elizabeth Zevenbergen. Great-Grandma Zevenbergen passed away when Stormi was fourteen. When Grandma died, there was a heart-shaped pendant of hers that went to my mom and dad's house for safekeeping until a later date for Stormi. Stormi didn't know anything about it until Ma Sue passed away just seven and a half weeks before the accident. We were at the church making arrangements for Ma Sue's funeral service when it was given to Stormi. I'll never forget the look on her face. It was one of surprise, grief, and happiness all at once. She was shocked because she didn't know it existed, grief-stricken because she was reliving losing Great-Grandma plus now losing Ma Sue, and happy because she was honored to have it. Stormi always tried to act all "big and tough" and didn't very often show her "crying" emotion, at least not to me. As we were leaving the church and she was walking to her car, I could see she was trying to shield her face, but I could see the tears running freely down her face. She would later tell me how much that pendant meant to her.

Who would have or could have known that just some eight weeks later Stormi would be holding that very pendant in her hands for all of eternity . . . in her own coffin.

Stormi was born on May 8, 1987, right on her due date, and came home from the hospital on Mother's Day. The fact that she came home at all was a mini miracle. I don't remember all the facts exactly, but it goes something like this: a drug that was given to her mother during delivery also got into Stormi's body. The drug suppressed Stormi's respiratory system and she didn't take that first big gulp of air that babies normally take upon birth. She didn't cry. She didn't do anything. Her heart was beating, but she wasn't breathing. They had called a pediatrician (thank God) into the delivery room prior to Stormi making her grand entrance. The pediatrician gave Stormi two or three shots in her thigh muscle to counteract the other drug. They even gave her some assisted breaths. It took what seemed like an eternity, but after a couple of minutes her breathing finally started. Her heart rate had even started to drop by that time. They told us when we took her home that there was no way of knowing for sure at that time, but there was a chance she had suffered some brain damage from being without oxygen for so long. I used to tease her that between that situation and being dropped on her head (she was *never* dropped) as a baby was the reason she ended up being a Minnesota Vikings fan instead of a Green Bay Packers fan like her dad. Life was a little scary at first, but we knew soon enough that she didn't have any brain damage, just attitude.

Unlike her sister, Jamie, who was born with a head full of thick, black hair, Stormi was born with red hair that wasn't very thick and it stuck up, so I called her my "little chick." Stormi was a year old before she slept through the night. That was my fault because I knew she was going to be our last child and I was gone all day at my construction job. So every time she would make the tiniest noise during the night, I would get up, make a bottle, grab Stormi from her crib, and sit in the rocking chair with her. It wouldn't take long and we both would be sleeping. We would stay there for an hour or so and then I would put her back in her crib. Finally her mother said, "Enough is enough," and put an end to it. It took a few nights of crying fits, but eventually it got better. Stormi got used to it too.

I don't know if it was her red hair or what, but Stormi was never short on "attitude." The terrible twos were just that—terrible. I remember one time when she didn't want to wear a coat into church. We never even made it into the sanctuary because she was screaming the whole time.

Her unwillingness to let anyone push her around or get in her way was demonstrated early in life. That became very apparent on one Sunday after we got home from church and Sunday school. It was after one of her first times going to the preschool class. If I remember right, it was for three—and four-year-olds. The class was taught by the same teacher I'd had when I was that age, and she taught for many years beyond Jamie and Stormi as well. Anyway, when we got home, I asked Stormi how it went, what she had learned. That was my first mistake. She proceeded to tell me she wasn't at all happy with the other kids because they wouldn't be quiet so she could listen. She went on and on about it.

Apparently I wasn't paying close enough attention to what she was saying because she raised her voice and said, "Dad, they really pissed me off." Mistake number two was letting her see me laugh.

Jamie and Stormi's mom and I got divorced when Stormi was in the second grade. I'm sure it's never an easy or good thing for any child to go through, but I think the girls adjusted well. I spent as much time as I could with the girls and had custody of them extra nights whenever possible. As the years went on, the girls even lived with me some of the time.

Stormi had never been a morning person. It was like pulling teeth to get her out of bed. I would try getting her to go to bed earlier at night, but she said it didn't help. When the girls lived with me, it was always a battle getting her up on the weeks it was her turn to use the bathroom first. She wanted to sleep in and have Jamie get up first. That, of course, wasn't fair to Jamie.

Stormi ended up with her own chair in the detention room in high school because she was always late. I don't know that she was ever late for work, but I'm sure she was never early either. She would call me and tell me how she had gotten up and made it to work on time in a matter of ten minutes. She would be just giggling as she told me because she knew how much it irritated me when she did that.

Part of her attitude was being bullheaded or headstrong. I would frequently have to have a conversation with her and explain that when she became the adult or the parent, she could make the rules. I told her that until that time she was to listen to the one in charge—parent, teacher, me, whomever. It would last a short period of time before she would need a reminder.

Her high school teachers would occasionally get a glimpse of her attitude. There was an occasion when she was involved in drama class and was in a play that she was also student directing. The play was performed once on each of two nights. I attended the play on the first night. There were a couple of occasions during the play where a number of students, including Stormi, had to recite some lines together. There were actually quite a few lines. I could hear Stormi quite well, but not so much the others. Stormi had a voice that carried well, but there was more to it than that—some of the others didn't know their lines as well as they should have. She found me after the play was done, and it only took about half a second to find out how upset she was. She thanked me for being there, apologized for what she called "a bad performance," gave me a hug and kiss, and headed off to the "after-play meeting." She said she was going to do some major chewing. Shortly after she walked away, the drama teacher came over to talk to me. She also thanked me for being there and asked if I had seen Stormi yet. I told her Stormi was a bit upset about the performance and was headed to talk to the others in the play. The teacher instantly got a terrified look on her face, excused herself, and headed right for the meeting. My guess is that she was going there to protect the other students from Stormi. I sure would have liked to have been a fly on the wall of that classroom. I was told that the next night's performance went much better and you could hear everyone's voice.

As I said before, Stormi was a huge Minnesota Vikings fan. I'm not sure why, but she was. I used to think maybe it was just to be different from me. Maybe it was because her favorite color was purple. Whatever the reason, she was a Vikings fan through and through. She knew the players, she knew the game, and she even went to some Viking games. Stormi *loved* the Vikings. My phone would ring every time the Vikings won—twice if the Packers lost. We would bet a soda pop whenever the two teams played each other. There was one of her high school teachers that she would also make a bet with on the Packer/Viking games. The loser would have to wear the opposing team's jersey at school on Monday. Her uncle and aunt had gone to an autograph signing by Matt Birk, the former center for the Vikings. They had him sign a football for her with her name on it and everything. It was meant to be a 2005 Christmas gift for her . . . instead it was displayed at her visitation and funeral. She never got to see it from this side of heaven. I still have it. There is a Vikings pennant buried with Stormi.

Stormi didn't always like being told what to do. She had a habit of keeping her cell phone with her in class even though the students were told to keep them in their locker or in their car. Also, she didn't always remember to turn it off or put it on silent. There was more then once that I had to go with her to the principal's office to "rescue" her phone. That usually led to another one of my "reminder conversations."

The day after one such rescue mission I decided to teach her a lesson. I knew what time the class was that usually got her into trouble, that she probably still had the phone with her, and that it was also probably still turned on. So I did the same thing that any loving dad would do—I called her. I was right on all counts. Man was she *mad*. But it was the last time I ever had to go rescue her phone. I always figured if the kids weren't mad at me at least part of the time, I was doing something wrong. I figured parent first, friend later—if I was lucky.

There was also the time I busted her leaving the school at noon. She liked going to Subway or McDonalds with friends at noon, and I liked her staying at the school so I knew where she was. I figured if she was at school, there was one less opportunity for her to get into an accident or trouble—you know teenagers. When I told her how I felt, she gave me the "but, Dad, all my friends go . . ." speech. I came right back with the "if your all friends jumped off of a cliff . . ." speech. I won, or at least I thought I did. After a period of time, "a little birdie" told me he had seen Stormi at Subway at noon on a school day. I questioned Stormi and she assured me she was staying at the school . . .

I decided to check it out for myself. I borrowed a friend's pickup, parked in the student parking lot, and waited. Sure enough, Stormi came walking out of the school, got in her car, and headed toward Subway. I stayed far enough back so she wouldn't see me, but that almost got me into trouble. I caught the start of a red light that was still green when she went through the intersection. Stormi didn't see me, but Mr. Police Officer did and I got pulled over. Thankfully it was an officer I knew, and when I explained why I was in such hurry, he told me to get going before she got away. Fortunately she had a red light at the next intersection and I caught up to her again. She pulled into the Subway parking lot and I pulled up right alongside her. The look on her face when I greeted her as she got out of her car was, to say the least, priceless. I can probably count on one hand the number of times she didn't have something to say, and this was one of them.

No matter how mad I was at the kids, I always ended the "discussion" with a hug, a kiss on the forehead, and an "I love you." This time was no different. I sent her into the restaurant to tell her friends that she wouldn't be joining them for lunch and then took care of the rest of the details outside. Even if I was mad at them, or they at me, I always wanted the girls to know how much they were loved in case we didn't get to see each other again. Less than a year later I found out just how important those hugs, forehead kisses, and "I love yous" are. Good times or bad, most often you truly don't know the last you might see a loved one.

Stormi graduated high school in May 2005. She didn't spend any time sitting around after that, and she worked two jobs. She worked at Ciatti's in Woodbury, Minnesota, and at the Hammond Hotel in Hammond, Wisconsin. The hotel used to be a working hotel many years ago but is now a restaurant and bar. Stormi worked as a server at both places. There were a lot of days she worked a double shift, working both places in the same day. Holding down two jobs helped her earn car payments, rent, living expenses, and fun money. I may be bragging a bit, but both girls were always hard workers and bought their own cars with their own money. Stormi had leased a brand new Saturn Ion around the time she graduated high school. She was so proud of her new car. Who could have known how things would end for her and the car she was so proud of?

In August 2005 she attended Century College in White Bear Lake, Minnesota. Even while attending school she worked at least one shift each day. She was studying psychology and political science. In case you hadn't gathered by now, Stormi was quite opinionated, so both subjects were right up her alley. She once talked about being a lawyer but said she didn't want to have to defend someone she knew was guilty. I thought it was great that she felt that way. She also once said she wanted to be the first women president. I jokingly asked her to please hurry so that she would beat "that other woman" (Hillary Clinton) who was talking about running for president at the time. Hmm . . . I wonder where Stormi got her opinionated personality from . . .

After her accident, some of Stormi's high school teachers and college professors told me that her opinions were one of the things they would really miss about her. One professor told me she really enjoyed Stormi's input during class discussions. I can only imagine. I miss many things about Stormi, but two of the things I miss most are her strong will and her opinions. There was conflict from time to time because of her personality, but that is part of what made Stormi, Stormi. I said it more than once that her name was a perfect fit. In some ways I liked the fact that she was so strong-willed. It made me feel a little more secure that she was heading out into the world and wasn't going to let people walk all over her. It may sound weird, but I miss the challenge of getting her to realize she needed to look at things from every side of the issue.

Just so you don't think Stormi was all "piss and vinegar," she did have a soft side as well. She was always willing to help someone out and was friends with most everyone. I found out at her visitation and funeral just how many friends she had. She had a smile that could light up a room. She acted like a clown and loved hamming it up. She was my youngest and made the most of it. She would sit on my lap every chance she got. On Thanksgiving Day, just one day before her accident, she sat on my lap at Dad's house after we were done with dinner and announced to everyone that she had told people at a baby shower the Saturday prior that she looked like me. My chest instantly puffed up with pride. My anticipation was high. Was it our eyes, our noses—what was it? Then she announced what she had told people I didn't even know. She said she looked like me, "Because we both have chicken legs, no butt, and a gut." The sound of rushing air was the breath leaving my puffed-up chest.

Stormi had gone to visit her great-grandpa Zevenbergen just three days before her accident. She stopped at his apartment and told him she was working a double that day and was visiting between the two jobs. She said she only had fifteen minutes to spend but wanted to spend it with him. She sat on his lap and they talked for the fifteen minutes. She called me on her way to work after the visit and told me she had stopped there to say hi and wanted to make sure that he was doing okay after losing his daughter, Ma Sue. He would later tell me how much that visit had meant to him.

Stormi left me a message on my cell phone a couple of weeks after Ma Sue passed away. She was crying during the message and told me I'd better not let anything happen to me because she couldn't live without me too. When I called her to find out what had prompted that, she said she had started thinking about losing Ma Sue and my blood scare, and it got the better of her. Told you she had a soft side. I think about that message quite often. I wish I had saved it; it would be nice to hear her voice telling me to not let anything happen to me. Isn't it ironic how things can turn around so quickly? She was worried about me . . .

Stormi changed some of her college schedules after Ma Sue passed away. She did that so she could go to the homeless shelter with Dad on Thursday afternoon/evenings so he wouldn't have to go alone. All of the grandkids had gone along with Mom and Dad at one time or another, especially at Christmas time, and really enjoyed it. After Dad and Stormi got done at the shelter, they would go to Menards and she would push the shopping cart around for him. She would call me that night or the next day and tell me how much fun they'd had and how much she enjoyed being with Grandpa, and Dad would tell me the same. Later, Dad not only lost his wife and a granddaughter in eight weeks' time, he lost his companions for going to the homeless shelter.

Stormi wrote the following entry on the Caring Bridge website just four days before Ma Sue passed away. People posted entries directed to the family, and some were directed to Mom. At the time Stormi wrote it, we were still hopeful things would turn around for our beloved Ma Sue. As I said before, we have always been a close family and I think this letter from Stormi goes to show some of that, as well as some of Stormi's own softness.

It goes as follows.

"My Beautiful Ma Sue—

"So this is my first time writing to you on here . . . I come and talk to you as often as I can get up here between school and work. I've always known you were a wonderful person and that everyone else thought so too, but the amount of people who check on you through this site (thank you, Ms. Jody!), the people who come to see you, and the tons and tons of cards you have gotten is unbelievable. I know you can pull through this; it just takes some trying and praying. God is always watching you and helping you to come back to be the fantastic wife, mother, and grandmother that you are. But more than anything, Ma Sue, you are a great friend to everyone! Grandpa loves you so much; the two of you are so blessed to have one another. Don't worry, I'm keeping Daddy in line (he thinks it's the other way around though, but we know better!). Everyone is doing well aside from some major heartache.

"It kills me to see you like this, Ma Sue . . . . But I can deal with it as long as I know you'll be better. I'm going to stop writing and go kiss you goodnight.

"My love, thoughts, and prayers are with you always.

"Love you lots, Ma Sue.

"Your Stormi Liz."

I remember the first time I read that letter after Stormi was gone. I cried until my eyes hurt. As strong-willed as she was, she was a soft-hearted person too. There are so many twists and turns to life, and to death. You just never know when you say, do, or write something if, how, or when it's going to affect people. It might be that day, it might be a month later, it might even be after you're gone . . .

Dad got back from Africa the day before Thanksgiving. Originally he had cancelled the trip when Mom's health continued to fail. A couple of weeks after her passing, Mom and Dad's friends who were also scheduled to go called and asked if I thought they should call Dad and again ask him to go. I said I thought it was a good idea but that they should check with my siblings to see what they thought. Everyone agreed Dad should go. It took a little convincing, but he went. I can understand his hesitation. He was understandably mourning the loss of Mom and it would be hard to go without her. It was a trip they had planned for a couple of years. Dad and the other couple left on November 4 and returned on the twenty-third.

Dad still managed to put together a Thanksgiving dinner even though he was only home for one day. Everyone helped out by bringing something, but it was Dad pulling it all together. It sure was strange and hard without Mom. Mom always put so much into family gatherings. She would work into the wee hours of the morning getting meals or birthday cakes ready. By morning her hands were so swollen from the arthritis she could hardly move them.

We did the best we could without Mom. There were a few tears, of course, but we got through it. We ate, sat around and talked, and watched football just like we did other years. The only thing missing was Mom. Stormi and her cousin Ashley were lying on the floor at one point and got their younger cousins to give them backrubs. When it came time for "payment" for the backrubs, Stormi sent the younger ones to get the payment from her daddy.

One of those same younger cousins was walking around with a digital camera that day. She didn't have a clue how it worked and had to ask a couple of times how to operate it. Her dad, my brother Jerry, didn't realize until a couple of weeks later that some pictures had actually been taken and stayed on the camera. Some of those pictures included pictures of Stormi Liz. They are the last pictures ever taken of her. What a blessing. How could anyone have known that an eight—or nine-year-old having fun with a camera could end up taking such treasured pictures? You have to wonder sometimes how many things in life have a reason behind them. Was it just luck that a camera was being played with that day? Was it just luck that pictures actually got taken and didn't all get erased that day? Was it just luck that Jerry didn't clear the camera without checking it first?

He didn't even know there was anything on it. Whatever the case, I'm grateful it happened.

We finished up our time together, and the girls said it was time for them to get going. They said their goodbyes to everyone and I walked them to the door. As always, I gave them hugs, told them I loved them, and gave them their kisses. Jamie always wanted two kisses, one on each cheek. Stormi was content with one kiss right on the forehead. I closed the door behind them, walked to the window, and watched them walk to their cars. It was the last time I saw Stormi alive. It was the last time I touched her skin . . . when it was warm. It was the last time I ever got to see her beautiful smile. I didn't talk to her on Friday, so it was the last time I ever talked to her. I have replayed those few moments a million times over in my mind.

The next time I saw Stormi Liz, they were doing CPR.

Stormi had worked two shifts on Friday the twenty-fifth, the day after Thanksgiving. I'm not sure if both shifts were at Ciatti's, but I do know that at least the second one was. She left work and went to a nearby liquor store in Woodbury to buy some wine. She was only eighteen. The legal age for drinking or buying, anything with alcohol is twenty-one. She used a fake ID.

The fake ID . . . here's something parents need to watch out for. I knew nothing of this until the accident happened. Underage kids find someone who is of age and has a fairly close resemblance to themselves. They then pay that person to "lose" their driver's license. Then all the of-age person has to do is go to the DMV, pay a small fee to replace the "lost" license, and get a new one. The underage person uses his or her usual license for driving but now has a "new identity" when needed. If anyone questions the resemblance, the underage drinker can always tell the person checking the ID that she changed her hair color or gained/lost a few pounds. I'm told it works like a charm, and it certainly did for Stormi. From what I was told it had worked more than once. Maybe it's something that's been done for years and I was just naïve. I don't know. A word of warning to people who decide to "lose" their licenses to "help" someone younger out: you can face criminal charges if things go terribly wrong!!

Stormi was no angel. She was like any other teenager/young adult. It was a holiday weekend, friends were home from college . . . it was party time. I had just had a discussion with her two weeks prior about underage drinking and the trouble she could get in, or worse. I had talked to her about driving while tired after working a double or going to school and working the same day. I think the conversation, like a lot of conversations with teenagers, fell on deaf ears.

Stormi headed for a house outside Baldwin where a bunch of her friends had gathered for a party. I have always been vocal about adults letting someone else's minor children drink at their home. I have always hated that, and I hate it even more now. The fact remains, though, that Stormi bought her own wine with a fake ID. Nobody forced it on her; she drank it herself. There's no one to blame for that but Stormi herself. The residents of the home didn't "pull the trigger" and cause Stormi's death, but they certainly helped to "load the gun" by providing a "safe house" for her to drink in. Ultimately,

Stormi didn't do anything that a lot of others haven't done at one time or another, but it cost her big time. She paid with her life.

Stormi kept telling the other kids at the party that she was tired and needed to get home. She was tired from working all day, and she needed to be at work in Hammond at 7:30 the next morning. She left the party shortly after 12:20 a.m. One of her girlfriends didn't see her leave and called her cell phone to say goodnight. They had a two-minute phone conversation from 12:24 to 12:26. The conversation was complete; we just don't know if Stormi was driving at the time of the call or was still in the driveway of the residence.

At 12:32, a text message came into Stormi's phone. It was never opened. She had already crashed . . . she had only made it three and a half miles from the party.

We don't know how Stormi's accident started, but we know how it ended. Stormi was driving westbound, headed for her mom's house in Hammond. Her car crossed the eastbound lane and entered the ditch on the south side of the road. Why she crossed over is what we don't know. Did she fall asleep? Did she drop her phone on the floor when she finished her conversation? Did she reach for her phone when the text message came in? We don't know the reason and I guess it ultimately doesn't make much difference. Whatever the reason, the time she would have had to react to the situation was compromised because she had been drinking wine.

What we do know: approximately one hundred fifty feet from where her car entered the south ditch was a crossroad. Her car clipped a stop sign, hit the crossroad, and became airborne. While airborne, her car brushed the side of a power pole on the opposite (west) side of the cross road. Her car was eight and a half to nine feet above the road surface at the time. The ditch was a good three feet deep in that area, so that put her car about twelve feet above the ground. To this day there are still scrape marks on that power pole. Her car traveled a little better than one hundred feet through the air. It came down nose first, flipping and rolling a number of times before coming to a rest. While all of that was bad enough, there is one other important detail: she *wasn't* wearing her seatbelt. Friends of hers would later tell me they didn't understand that because, they said, she always wore it. It really doesn't make much difference if she normally did or not, she wasn't wearing it when she needed it most. Stormi didn't have her seatbelt on, she was probably using her cell while driving, she was driving while tired, she was speeding, and she had been drinking. In other words, she didn't do one thing right that night.

Stormi stayed with or in her car until its last roll. She was ejected and gently placed on the ground eight and a half feet from her car. It may sound weird to say "ejected" and "gently" in the same sentence, but that's what happened. There were a lot of details about the accident that got explained in the investigation by the state patrol.

Stormi was "warm-blooded" like me. She often didn't wear a heavy coat, no matter how cold it was. That night she was wearing a short-sleeved shirt with an unbuttoned, long-sleeved shirt over it. That's the way she was found, wearing only two shirts, jeans, and shoes. It was only twelve degrees that morning.

Stormi was found the next morning by two deer hunters driving down the road headed for their hunting spot. They saw her car in the ditch and got out to investigate. They found Stormi . . . it was only twelve degrees out.

She was lying face down in an inch or two of snow. They put a blanket over her . . . it was only twelve degrees.

The accident happened between 12:26 a.m. and 12:32 a.m., and it was now almost 7:10 a.m. . . . it was only twelve degrees.

My pager went off for a car accident with ejected female occupant, found unconscious, but with arms moving . . . it was only twelve degrees.

Stormi's heart stopped about the same time they were loading her into the ambulance . . . she was only eighteen.

I pulled myself together and waited for the room to stop spinning. I couldn't believe my eyes. They were doing CPR on my daughter, my Stormi Liz. This couldn't be real, I had to be dreaming, it had to be a really bad nightmare. But it wasn't a nightmare, it *was* real, and it *was* happening. The room was full of people: doctors, nurses, fellow EMTs. The hallway was also full: nurses, more EMTs, police. A couple of the EMTs were crying. CPR and crying EMTs—that's never a good combination. Being an EMT can be a stressful job, and doing CPR can be emotional, especially when it involves someone young. It makes matters worse when it involves the child of someone you know. And on top of that, the father of that child is now standing there watching CPR in progress. CPR not being performed by doctors or nurses but by my fellow EMTs themselves. How would it be possible for them to not be stressed or emotional?

I had been standing in the doorway of the emergency room but then started to walk into the room. Out of concern, one of the EMTs tried to stop me from going in. He was stopped by the Baldwin ambulance director, who told him to let me go. I appreciated the concern, but there was no way he was stopping me.

What had only been a matter of seconds to this point seemed like an eternity. There were a lot of people next to Stormi, but I squeezed in. I touched her skin; it was cold as ice. I held her hand, but I was the only one doing any holding; her hand didn't move. I couldn't believe this was happening. She looked fine. She had little pieces of grass in her hair, a little scrape on her nose, and a little cut on her left pinky finger. That's it, that's all there was. She looked fine, so why were they doing CPR? I guess I don't know what I thought I should see, but I was thinking she should have had more obvious injuries for them to be doing CPR. I had certainly seen some horrible things in my years as an EMT because of car accidents, and some of those people survived just fine *without* CPR. I was trying to be a dad and an EMT at the same time, and it wasn't working.

I was asked a lot of questions by the hospital staff. Questions about allergies, medical history, medications, those kind of questions. Then a police officer came in and asked a question. He asked me if the person lying on the bed was Stormi Elizabeth Hielkema. I thought that was the stupidest question I had ever heard. Of course it was Stormi, who else would it be? Why else would I be standing there crying and holding her hand? That's when I found out. That's when I found out about the fake ID. Thank God for Small Town, USA. Thank God the EMTs and rescue personal at the scene of the accident knew it was Stormi. Otherwise, how long would it have been before I was notified? Would another family have been notified that their daughter had been in an accident? Word of warning to you kids out there with an ID with someone else's name on it: what if you need *immediate* medical attention and the hospital staff, police, whoever can't figure who you are? Or worse yet, what if family members need to be notified of a death? Do you want someone else's family to receive "the call?" Think about it!

I continued to stand next to Stormi. I held her hand and told her she could do this, she could make it. I reminded her how strong-willed she was. The doctors ordered more medications, medications that would help to get her heart started. I reminded her of how she got the shots right after birth to get her breathing going.

They said that her core temperature was down to eighty-four degrees. I wondered how that could be. I didn't yet know if she had been out in the cold for seven minutes or almost seven hours. I asked one of the doctors what her chances were. He said her low core temperature would maybe help, that maybe it had slowed everything down so that she had a chance. That's when I looked. That's when I lifted her eyelids and looked. I looked to see what her pupils were like. That's also when I knew. I knew she wasn't going to make it. I didn't give up hope, but I knew she wouldn't be coming home. Her pupils were dilated and nonreactive. They didn't react to light. In other words, there wasn't any brain activity. EMTs know nothing compared to a doctor, but right about that time, I was wishing I didn't even know the little I did know. I looked over and saw that one of the doctors had seen me checking her pupils. He lowered his head ever-so-slightly. He knew I knew.

I now knew the completely helpless feeling Dad had felt thirty years prior. How he and Mom must have felt standing next to me in the emergency room of the hospital not knowing if I was going to survive. How Dad felt that he "should have been there." I think that moment was about the worst of all. I lost it. I had been crying before this, but now I lost it. An arm came from somewhere and steadied me, held me. I have no idea whose arm it was, but I needed it.

As I stood there, I started to wonder. I wondered if Stormi was "somewhere in between." I wondered if she was "floating" around the room the way I had. They were doing CPR. Was her soul already gone? When does the soul leave? When the doctor says you're dead or when God says you are? There wasn't a crucifix on the wall that she could go to like I did so that she wasn't hurting or scared. I found myself wishing there was. I knew I wasn't going to see her, but I looked around the room for her just the same. Twice in fewer then eight weeks time of standing next to a loved one and "looking" for them was more than I could take.

Some other family members had arrived now, including Dad. I'll never forget the look of complete devastation on his face. He had just buried his wife, and now here laid one of his grandchildren, his new homeless shelter partner. I have always considered Dad to be a very strong person, but I wondered how much more he could take, how much more any of us could take.

The helicopter was there now, ready to fly her to Regions Hospital in St. Paul, Minnesota. Regions is a major trauma hospital. They placed her on the stretcher to take her to the helicopter, all the while doing CPR. One of the smaller EMTs was asked to fly with her to help assist CPR, and I was told there wasn't room for me.

I went out in the hallway while they were getting her ready for the chopper. There was more confusion out there, questions by the police. Even though it was being paid for by Stormi, her new car was registered in her mother's name because leases are harder for young people to get started. Now they were wondering if someone else could have been involved because there was yet a third last name. I explained to them that name belonged to Stormi's mom. That cleared up that mess.

The police now had a few details. They knew Stormi had been to a house party the night before and that she had left around 12:15 or so. The house where she had been was fewer than four miles from where the accident was. I still don't know how they found that out so quickly, but they did. I added up the number of hours in my head: almost seven hours. Seven hours in twelve degree cold. Now it made sense why her core temperature was so low. I lost it again.

I realized Stormi had been wheeled down the hallway and was headed for the helicopter pad, and I ran to catch up. I got to the door just as they were loading her into the chopper, CPR still going. They didn't waste any time and took off immediately. I stood and watched from as close to the fence around the pad as I could get. The wind coming off the rotors of the helicopter was incredibly cold. The snow and ice being kicked up from the ground around the pad felt like tiny razors hitting my face. I didn't care.

It was only twelve degrees out . . .

Stormi was only eighteen . . .

Jamie was at the hospital now too. She had driven there from her apartment in Hudson. She knew Stormi had been in a bad car accident, but that's about all she knew. Jamie and Stormi weren't just sisters, they were best friends. In fact, they often said that they were "better then best friends." They had their differences growing up of course, but now they did pretty much everything together. In fact, they were supposed to go job hunting together the day of the accident. The Ciatti's in Woodbury where they both worked was going to be closing its doors. They both wanted to find a new serving job at the same place and work together again. You can imagine the emotions when Jamie found out Stormi was now in a helicopter receiving CPR.

Four of us, including Jamie, headed for Regions Hospital in my car. There were other vehicles full of family members headed there as well. God must have decided I didn't need to be bothered by police that day because I drove between ninety and ninety-five mph the whole way and never saw a single police car. They would have had to have given me the ticket at the hospital because there was no way I was going to stop. It is approximately forty miles to Regions, and other than the first one and a half miles and the last block, it was all interstate driving. That made it a lot easier and safer to drive that fast.

The car wasn't the only thing racing on the way to the hospital—so was my mind. I kept replaying the sights and sounds in the emergency room in Baldwin. The CPR, the condition of her pupils, her core temperature, her lifeless hands, the hum of voices from the doctors and nurses. I had learned a little bit about hypothermia in EMT class, how body systems can actually survive because they were "preserved" by the cold. I daydreamed how Stormi could be one of the few to survive because of being so cold. I had visions of getting to the hospital and finding Stormi sitting up in bed wondering what all the fuss was about. Then I remembered her pupils . . . I prayed . . . I prayed . . . I prayed.

We parked in a parking lot that was right in front of the emergency room area of Regions. We ran into the hospital and up to the attendant at the reception desk. I blurted out who we were and what we were there for. I said we needed to get to the emergency room where Stormi was. The attendant said we needed to get name tags from security first. I said no, there wasn't time for that. A security guard nicely but firmly said that no one was going anywhere without name tags. I asked how Stormi was, and either no one knew the answer or they wouldn't say. It seemed like an eternity, but it actually didn't take that long to get the tags. The security guard then led us back to the emergency rooms. We walked, walked, and walked some more, or at least it seemed like we did. We walked right past all kinds of emergency rooms. I didn't understand. Where was she? I had the vision again of getting to her room and finding her sitting up in bed with that big beautiful smile of hers. Finally we were there, but this room had a door. The other emergency rooms all had curtains in front of them. I didn't understand.

The security guard opened the door to the room. Instead of finding Stormi lying in a bed, there were other people in there. Her mother was there, her maternal grandparents, an uncle and aunt, cousins. I wondered, *Where is Stormi, and who is with her?* My dad and some other family members arrived right behind us. Everyone was standing. I felt like we were cattle being herded into a pen. The security guard said the doctor would be right in. I asked again how Stormi was, and he repeated that the doctor would be right in.

It seemed like everything was moving in slow motion, but soon enough the door opened. As it turned out, anytime the door would have opened was too soon. I don't even remember how many people walked in. I know there were at least two, a female doctor and another lady. I remember that the doctor was a tall woman. The doctor asked if Stormi's parents were there, and we identified ourselves. For the next few minutes everything is a blur. I remember hearing, "We did everything we could, but Stormi didn't survive her injuries." There were gasps, there were screams, and there were, of course, tears.

I said I wanted to see my daughter. We were led down a short hallway to what they called a bereavement room. I had never heard of such a thing as a bereavement room, a room just for spending time with a loved one who has passed away. The door was opened and there lay my beautiful baby girl, my Stormi Liz. She was covered with a sheet except for her head and her left hand. I took her hand in mine. From behind me I heard Jamie twice scream Stormi's name at the top of her lungs. I couldn't take it anymore, and I lost it too.

As the next better than three hours went on, more family members arrived at the hospital. It was the most incredibly difficult time you could ever imagine. There were a lot of hugs and even more tears. You would have thought we were all out of tears after losing Ma Sue only seven and a half weeks before. Not even close. We had spent some time with Ma Sue after she was gone, but this was different. We knew the end was coming for Mom so we had a chance to say some goodbyes ahead of time. Stormi's death was completely unexpected. How do you deal with something like that?

I still couldn't understand that Stormi didn't just get up off of that bed and walk out of the room. There was just the scrape on the end of her nose and the little cut on her left pinky finger. Those were all the injuries you could see. There were, of course, her cold, lifeless hands. I couldn't believe how cold her skin was. I knew she had been out in the twelve-degree cold for almost seven hours, but I thought she would have started to warm up some. I stayed close to her as much as I could, but others needed to be close to her as well. I picked some of the pieces of grass out of her hair.

There was one thing that made it believable that she was gone—the intubation tube. Most times when a person is receiving CPR in a professional setting, she is intubated. That means there is a tube in her mouth, which goes down into the trachea and assures proper air flow when she is being given "breaths." The tube typically sticks out of the patient's mouth a couple of inches. Even though a person has been declared dead by a doctor, the tube has to stay in place until the coroner arrives and agrees with the doctor's determination. In Stormi's case, the coroner wasn't brought in until the family was done spending their time with her. In other words, the tube was there the whole time we were. I have seen that tube left in place a number of times over the years, but never of course on my own child. I had to explain a number of times to additional family members as they arrived why the tube had to stay in place. It made a difficult situation even more difficult for some of the family, and I didn't like it either.

A hospital chaplain came by and offered to say a prayer. There's a job you couldn't give me, trying to comfort people who have just lost a loved one. There are those who would welcome a chaplain at this point, but you have to know the last person some people are going to want to talk to after losing a loved one is a "man of God." I have to be honest. God wasn't exactly at the top of my list at that moment either. First He takes a sixty-three-year-old woman getting ready for a mission trip, and then an eighteen-year-old young woman with her whole life in front of her. Both gone forever in just seven and a half weeks' time. And oh yeah, one is my *mom*, the other is my *daughter*. This poor chaplain had his work cut out for him. I talked with him for a while and expressed my frustrations. As we talked I realized it wasn't his fault Stormi was lying there. I also realized he wasn't just doing his job, he cared about us and about the life that had been lost. I decided a prayer would be fine. He did a nice job with the prayer, but God had some major explaining to do.

Even though Stormi's eyes were closed, a cool, damp washcloth had been lain over them to help keep them moist. We were told that would help keep them in better condition for donation purposes should we choose to do that. That only added to the difficulty of the situation. There lay my daughter, lifeless, a tube sticking out of her mouth, and now a damp cloth on her eyes. Thing was, I knew it was going to get worse from there, much worse.

We all spent time in the bereavement room with Stormi. There ended up being enough people so that not everyone could fit in the room at the same time, so I spent some time out in the hallway as well. There were people to call to let them know what had happened, and I did that from there. I needed to get away from it all from time to time, so I went on some walks. I walked outside wearing just jeans and an insulated shirt. It was still cold out, and I wanted to try to imagine what Stormi had gone through. I was out there for ten or fifteen minutes, Stormi for almost seven hours—not much of a comparison, is it? I walked because she couldn't. I walked a lot over the course of the next few weeks for that reason. I would sit for just a short time and then be up walking again, even if it was just back and forth in a room. I guess it was my first way of coping. Half the battle of losing a child is figuring out a way to cope with the loss, a way that works for you. Everyone is different; what works for one only makes it worse for the next person. It has to be what works for you.

Anger started to build in me. How could this have happened? What role, if any, did alcohol play in the accident? I didn't yet know what kind of alcohol Stormi had bought, but I knew she had bought her own to drink. Who was the person who gave Stormi her new "identity" so that she was able to buy it? What gave someone the right to let *my* minor child drink in *their* home and then allow her to drive? How could she have laid out there for almost seven hours in twelve-degree weather and nobody saw her? Questions needed to be answered.

I can't begin to explain the complete, totally helpless feeling I felt. There lay one of my children, one of my dreams for the future, and there wasn't a thing I could do about it. Nothing. Besides the obvious utter devastation of losing Stormi, I think that helpless feeling was about the worst. There wasn't a little scrape on her knee from falling off her bike that I could kiss and make better. There wasn't a boy who had hurt her feelings and I could make her smile by threatening to beat him up. I couldn't fix this. Dads are supposed to be able to fix *everything*. There's not nearly enough letters in the word "helpless" to be to describe the feeling I had.

There were a lot of decisions to be made, difficult ones. Someone from the hospital asked me where we wanted Stormi's body sent. *Body?* That's my *daughter*, not a body. That was just one of many reality face slaps to come. With Stormi's mother's approval, it was decided that the O'Connell Funeral Home in Baldwin would handle the arrangements for Stormi's service. They had done such a wonderful job of helping us with Ma Sue. I couldn't believe that after such a short period of time we were going to be spending time there again. The O'Connells are wonderful people and have a beautiful new facility, but I hated that place.

Next was the autopsy. They said that before Stormi was brought back to Baldwin, they would be performing an autopsy. I said an autopsy wouldn't be necessary. I thought an autopsy was an optional thing, something her family could decide to have done or not. She'd had a car accident, she hadn't survived—what more did we need to know? Truth of the matter is, I knew a little of what happened during an autopsy . . . not happening on my daughter. I knew she wouldn't be able to feel it, it wouldn't hurt, I just didn't see the point. It's not like they were taking organs to help someone else at that point. I spent fifteen minutes on the phone begging the doctor whose office was responsible for autopsies not to do one. He said that for various reasons, it was in the best interest to know what injuries took her life.

I wondered for whose or what best interest. I lost, and an autopsy was to be performed. Reality slap number two.

Stormi had the "donor" sticker on her driver's license. She had talked some over the years about wanting to donate if the time ever came. Well, the time was here. The hospital staff said she wouldn't be able to donate organs because they have to be "harvested" right after death. The person has to be clinically alive just before the procedure is started. For that reason they said Stormi didn't qualify for organs, but she did for other things. I spent more than half an hour on the phone with the donation people. They asked what seemed like a million medical questions. Not just about her, but about her family too. I guess that makes sense; you wouldn't want someone with diseases or in their family history donating organs or tissue. They gave me the options of what she qualified for. Stormi ended up donating her eyes, skin off her thighs and back for burn victims, tendons and ligaments from her knees for people having reconstructive surgery, and her thigh (femur) bones for people with badly broken legs or bone cancer. They offered to harvest every other rib and the bones in her forearms as well. I said no to those. I didn't know what clothes she would wearing in her coffin, so I said no to the forearms. I didn't want scars on her arms in case she was wearing something with short sleeves. I said no to the ribs because I felt I needed to draw the line somewhere. There was going to be enough cutting . . . there was the autopsy, my little girl . . . slap number three.

It was time to leave, but it was *so* hard to go. In some ways it was such a strange thing to be doing, spending that much time with someone who is no longer living. But how could you not? How could a parent not stay with his child given the opportunity? It was the hardest thing I had done in my life to that point. I knew it was going to be exceeded in the coming days.

One by one we left the room after saying goodbye to Stormi . . . goodbye for the moment. I made it just a little ways down the hallway when I realized she was in the room by herself. I couldn't stand the thought of that. I went back in with her until someone from the hospital staff was able to be with her until she was moved. I told her how much I loved her and that I was sorry for not being there to help her. I again thought about how Dad must have felt thirty years earlier when he said he should have been there. I knew in my head that nothing would have changed in either case, but my head wasn't talking, my heart was. I said one last goodbye for the moment, gave her the kiss on the forehead that she always liked, and left the room.

As we were leaving, Stormi's mom asked if I could stop at her house and help explain to Stormi's nine-year-old brother and four-year-old sister that Stormi wasn't going to be coming home . . . ever. A neighbor had gone over to be with them, and they had no idea yet what had happened. Those reality face slaps were really starting to hurt.

On the way to Hammond where Stormi's mom lives, it was decided to stop in Hudson and see Stormi's car. It was sitting in the impound yard of the St. Croix County Sheriff's Department. It may seem like a strange to do, to see the car that your daughter crashed in and died as a result of that crash only hours earlier, but it was something I needed to do. I don't know, maybe it would make it seem more real. Maybe it would make it more understandable why she was lying in a bed in the bereavement room of a hospital instead of working her job at the Hammond Hotel.

The gate to the impound yard was locked when we got there, but her car was within ten feet or so of the fence. The driver's side was next to the fence. I don't know what I was expecting, but I guess what I saw wasn't it. Her car had plenty of damage, but not as much as I thought it would. Of course I didn't know many details of the accident itself yet, just that she had been ejected from the car. I guess I was thinking that if someone was ejected from a car, there must be pretty much nothing left of it. Deep down I knew that wasn't true, all that was needed was a door to pop open or window to be broken out. Her car was missing some of its windows. I stood there for a brief moment thinking about how proud she was to have that car, about how hard she had worked to get it.

As I looked closer, I saw what appeared to be much more significant damage on the passenger side. I just couldn't get around the fenced area to see it. One thing really caught my attention. There were papers stuck between the driver's door and the car itself, at the top of the door. They were stuck in there like when you see someone going down the road with their seatbelt hanging out. I couldn't figure out how they had gotten there or why at the top of the door. I would learn soon enough what that was all about. It would end up explaining why she only had the scrape on her nose and the cut on her finger. It would end up explaining what took her life. It would end up being what has tormented me ever since.

We got to Hammond and did our best to explain to Stormi's younger brother and sister what had happened to her. How do you explain something like that to a nine—and four-year-old, especially the four-year-old? How much do they understand about life and death? I didn't even understand it myself. After my "somewhere-in-between" experience, I thought life was going to run smoothly until everyone was really old and gray. First Ma Sue, now Stormi. I didn't understand myself, so how much help was I when explaining?

We went into Stormi's bedroom. It looked pretty much like I expected: messy. To her, there was no sense in putting clothes in a dresser when there was a perfectly good floor right next to it. It actually made me smile a bit because it was Stormi Liz the way I remembered her being when she lived with me. The smile didn't last long though; there were a lot of tears in that room. In her room were some of the things I had given her over the years. The little figurines, the Breyer Horses she collected for a number of years. There were pictures: family ones, friend ones, pictures of high school graduation only six months before.

Then I found something lying on top of a clothes basket, something that has helped me get through this about as much as anything: a pair of Minnesota Vikings sweatpants. It was the sweatpants I had seen her wear a thousand times. It's what she wore sitting around the house. It's what she wore to bed at night. She would have lived in them if she could. With her mom's permission, I took them. I held them as tight as I could; those sweatpants became my new "security blanket." For the next few weeks they were never more than a stone's throw from me. It was my connection to her for the time being. It made me feel as close to her as possible considering the circumstances. It reminded me of how big a Vikings fan she was and how much fun we used to have with the Packers/Vikings feud. It was another way of coping. There's no way to prepare for the loss of a child. Finding releases such as a "security blanket" make it a little more bearable. Finding what works for you is the tricky part.

I cried myself to sleep that night, just like I did for many nights to come. My new "blankie" was held tightly in my hands. It caught some of the tears, but there was nothing that could catch all of them.

The next few days were a living hell. Stormi's death wasn't something I could run and hide from. It wasn't going to go away. There were *a lot* of things that needed to be taken care of.

The news of Stormi's death spread like wildfire. There were already food items sitting on the front steps of the house when we got home that day. Over the course of the next couple of weeks, it was amazing how many people stopped by with food items, offers to help with anything and everything, condolences and hugs. The phone was equally busy. I was overwhelmed by how many cards came in the mail. It was all greatly appreciated. There have been times over the years when I have been less than excited about living in a small town where everyone knows everyone else's business. This was one time I was happy to be living there. I couldn't go anywhere without someone stopping me to offer condolences and a handshake or hug. Some people might not like that and feel as though they are constantly being reminded of what happened, but I was just the opposite. I knew all too well what had happened, so someone saying something didn't make it any worse. I appreciated that they took the time to say something. I understand that it's not an easy thing to do, to come up with something to say to someone who has just lost a child. I've lived through it, and I still don't always know what to say to someone who is experiencing the same pain. Sometimes a handshake or hug says everything that needs to be said.

I had never been involved in the planning of a funeral prior to Ma Sue's. This was going to be different yet again. While making Ma Sue's arrangements, Dad was ultimately the decision maker and my siblings and I were the "assistants." Only now I had "graduated." I wasn't an assistant anymore, and I didn't like it. It seemed so horribly wrong to have the time span of a whole pregnancy to plan for the arrival of a child but only a few days to plan for the burial of one. Actually, there was only a day or two available to make the arrangements because the funeral would be taking place in a few days. For obvious reasons it wasn't easy to think straight and I wanted to be thinking clearer than ever. It may sound strange to say, but I wanted Stormi's funeral to be every bit as meaningful as the day she was born. I felt I owed her that.

A good part of Sunday was spent planning Stormi's funeral. We met with the staff at the O'Connell Funeral Home. It seemed like we had just walked out their doors. It was decided that her funeral service would take place in the church that she'd been baptized because the size of the church building where she'd been confirmed and was a member of was too small for the crowd we anticipated. Her funeral service would be in the same church she'd started Sunday school in but hadn't liked the way the other kids were talking when she was trying to listen. It was the same church Ma Sue's funeral had been in just eight weeks earlier. The funeral service itself would be performed jointly by the pastor of the church where the service was being held and her mother's pastor.

It was decided to have the visitation on Tuesday from 4:00 to 9:00 p.m. at the funeral home. That's a longer time than some visitations, but we expected a lot of people and wanted to be prepared for it. As it turned out, that was a very good decision. The funeral service would be held on Wednesday at 10:30 a.m. Visitation would also be at the church one hour before the service and there would be a luncheon after the burial.

We called Sharon Freitag and asked her to sing for the service. Sharon can sing like no other—she could put 99 percent of the contestants on *American Idol* to shame. She accepted, saying she would be honored to sing for Stormi. Two songs were chosen. Stormi loved, "There's Holes in the Floor of Heaven," which would be the first song. The second would be "Jesus Loves Me," the same one Sharon sang for Stormi the day she was baptized. I loved the way she sang it during the baptism service. She sang while playing guitar and interjected Stormi's name in place of the word "me" throughout the song. It was absolutely beautiful. I knew it was going to be equally beautiful the second time around, just in a much different way. Kind of gave the term "bittersweet" a whole new meaning to me. How many people get to have the same person who sang at their baptism to sing at their funeral? But then again, how many would want that? That would mean the person doing the singing was old enough to sing at your baptism and still be alive and well enough to sing at your funeral. Long story short, the person being buried probably isn't very old.

A casket needed to be picked out. We decided on one that was as close to purple as we could find. Stormi loved the color purple. Growing up, it was the color of the walls in her bedroom, the carpet, the drapes, everything. And of course, there's the Vikings. The casket had a small drawer in it. The drawer was there so people could write letters to Stormi and have them buried with her. I didn't write one. I decided my eulogy would take the place of a letter. Jamie and their mother, Bonny, were to pick out what Stormi was going to be wearing for the rest of eternity in her casket. It was also decided to have Stormi hold the pendant from Great-Grandma Zevenbergen in her hands. We just needed to find where she'd put it.

Pallbearers needed to be chosen. It wasn't an easy thing to do because Stormi had a lot of friends. A mix of young men and women where chosen, six and two respectively. As each was called and asked if they would be one of Stormi's pallbearers, they all said they would be honored. Holly, who was one of her best friends and chosen to be a pallbearer, was in army boot camp in Missouri at the time. Because Stormi was not immediate family to Holly, there was a lot of red tape for her to go through to get back for the funeral, but she made it. It would have been very hard on Holly if she had not been able to get back.

The arrangements were all made—the arrangements for the funeral of an eighteen-year-old. I still couldn't believe it was true, but Stormi was gone. Not just gone away to school or something, but gone *forever*. The whole time we were at the funeral home, I held on to those Vikings sweatpants. I carried them everywhere those next days. I can't explain it, but they comforted me. Somehow they took the edge off just a little. As time went on, I would still take them with me when I went someplace, but I left them in the vehicle. As I said before, they came in handy for drying tears, and there were plenty of those.

So many things were going through my mind. I thought about all the things I would be missing with Stormi gone. I thought about how there would be a Saturday not quite four years down the road when I should have been sitting in an auditorium watching her graduate college. Three years after that she would have been done with graduate school. It had been a dream of mine since the day the girls were born to walk them down the isle on their wedding day. Stormi and I had had a conversation just a couple of weeks earlier about boys. She said, "Dad, I don't have time for that." She told me boys would have to wait till she was done with school. Whether she meant it, I'm not sure. Just the same, there would be a Saturday sometime down the road when I should have been walking her down the isle. Grandchildren? I can't wait for grandchildren. Anyone who knows me knows how much I love kids, especially babies. As much as I dreamt about walking the girls down the aisle someday, I looked forward to their children, my grandchildren, just as much. I have looked forward to sitting in the rocker or playing on the floor with grandchildren just as I did with the girls. "Spoil 'em rotten and send 'em home" was my plan for years. I thought about how sometime down the road, my phone should have rung in the middle of the night and Stormi would call me Grandpa instead of Dad. As a parent, you have so many dreams and daydreams for your children. This was the ultimate dream buster. I was grateful for the life there had been to this point but felt the worst kind of heartbreak about the lack of future life.

I felt *very* selfish for thinking about the things *I* would be missing. What about Stormi? She wasn't going to get to graduate from college . . . she wasn't going to get to fall in love . . . she wasn't going to get to walk down the aisle . . . she wasn't going to get to know the joy of having children . . . she wasn't going to have the thrill of buying her first home. She wasn't going to experience the joys in life that I had been able to. She had so much to offer this world. With her piss-and-vinegar personality, she would have gone places. Stormi missed out. The *world* missed out.

With the arrangements for the funeral service complete, one thing still needed to be done: a burial spot for Stormi needed to be chosen. Where to bury one of your children is something you don't ever think about, at least not until you have to. In a perfect world, I would have liked to have buried her next to where I would be buried someday. But it's not a perfect world. Her mother and I weren't married anymore and it wouldn't be fair to have her buried next to one of us and not the other. We decided to have her buried in the Baldwin cemetery as close to Ma Sue as possible. Immediately to the right of where Mom is buried, and where Dad will be, were two open plots. We knew the plots had originally been purchased by former farm neighbors of Mom and Dad, and for the same reason Mom and Dad had bought theirs—they had lost an infant daughter. They had purchased three plots and buried their daughter on the far right plot, keeping the other two for themselves. The last information we knew about the former neighbors was that they had moved to Iowa some thirty-five years or so earlier. Dad checked with the cemetery board and found that the plots were still owned by the same couple. He offered to try to track them down and see if they would be willing to sell the plots. With some leg work, phone calls, and the Internet, Dad found them, and thankfully they were willing to sell the plots. They sold them back to the cemetery board, and then in turn, Dad bought them from the board saying it was his gift to Stormi Liz. Now it was going to be Stormi, Ma Sue, Stormi's infant cousin, and infant aunt all buried together. Great-Grandma Zevenbergen is only thirty feet away. It was getting to be a little family area, one I didn't like very much.

On Monday I called the college Stormi attended and told them what had happened. The woman who answered the phone was most gracious and sincere. I gave her the website address for the funeral home so people could check on the arrangements if they wanted to. She said she would send a general e-mail to the whole college and a more specific one to Stormi's professors. It wouldn't take long at all to find out just how nice a person that woman was, as well many others from the college.

I also had to call the insurance agency where her car was insured. She had her own policy, but it was attached to mine to help her with rates. None of the calls that needed to be made regarding Stormi's death were easy, and this one was no different. I had to talk to adjusters as well as the agent. They had questions I didn't necessarily know the answer to, so I had to call the sheriff's department as well. I knew things weren't going to get any easier for a long time. I wondered if they ever would.

Even with the terrible, horrible thing that had happened, my construction business needed to keep going. My employees did a wonderful job taking work matters into their own hands so I could take care of family matters. I still went to the office a few times that week just to get out of the house. It didn't matter much were I went because the pain was everywhere I was.

A cross in the ditch. We've all seen one. A cross placed in the ditch along the side of a road as a memorial to someone who died at that location, or as the result of an accident that happened there. I've seen them along rural country roads in Wisconsin where I live. I've seen them along highway and interstate roads around the country. Sometimes it's a real simple cross, just two branches tied together. Sometimes it's one made out of hard foam, like the ones you see in a cemetery. Sometimes it's an elaborate one, painted nicely with a name or names on it. Occasionally there are even flowers planted around it, or fresh flowers brought there on "angelversary" dates.

Over the years there have been times when I've been driving along in an area where I haven't been before and have seen a cross. When I saw the cross I may have wondered what happened there, how old the person was . . . how *young* the person . . . how many people . . . mother . . . father . . . . grandparent . . . child? I may have offered up a little prayer for that person or their family, or I may have driven by and not given it much thought at all. There have been times around the area where I live that I have known the story behind the cross. I knew who died there and at least some of the circumstances of the accident that claimed their life.

No matter what I knew or didn't know about the stories behind crosses I have seen in the past, no matter what attention I did or didn't give that cross, there's now a cross out there that I know everything there is to know about, and the story behind it. It's a cross at the intersection of County Road E and 220th Street, three miles north and one mile east of Baldwin. It's a cross made of wood, a cross that sometimes has flowers by it, a cross that has a name on it. It's a cross that has the big, bold letters—S T O R M I—on it, the name of my daughter . . .

Holly wasn't the only friend of Stormi's to come back to Baldwin for her funeral. A couple of young men flew back from Colorado. The family home for one of these young men is only half a mile east of where the accident happened. There may have been others who came from afar that I am not aware of.

When the guys got back, they, along with another young man, took it upon themselves to build a cross for their friend Stormi. They built a very nice wooden cross for her, routing (carving) her name into the horizontal member. They even painted it, painting the inset of the letters a different color so her name would stand out better.

They put the cross up on Monday night, the night before the visitation. I wasn't there, but I'm told a lot of Stormi's friends were. I didn't know at the time that it was taking place, or I would have been there too. I think it's a wonderful tribute from her friends. Throughout this whole terrible ordeal, I was/still am greatly comforted by the friends Stormi had and the wonderful things they did and said.

The Kusilek family farm is only a few hundred yards from the intersection where the accident was. Every summer since the accident, the Kusileks have kept the weeds and grass mowed in the area around Stormi's cross. It's a large and sometimes wet area, and I'm sure they have to use farm machinery to mow it. It's not mowed like the yard around a house is, but it's kept plenty short so that her cross is clearly visible from the road. Once when I was thanking them for keeping it mowed, Mrs. Kusilek said she had "always wanted that area to look a little neater." Now, she said, "There is a reason to do so." It would be difficult for me to do what they do. It couldn't be done with a push mower, and I don't have a way to haul a riding mower there. I truly appreciate their kindness.

I have driven by Stormi's cross many times. Sometimes it's right on my way to where I'm going, sometimes not. I have driven by not slowing down much at all, just giving it a quick glance. There have been times I slowed way down, and there have been times I stopped and got out of the car. I have gone there when I'm having a good day just to "say hi." I have gone there when I'm having a crappy day just to remind myself how lucky I am to still be here and can have crappy days. Is it weird to be thankful for crappy days? I don't think so; at least I still have them. I know in heaven all of Stormi's days are good ones, but I would prefer she was here having some crappy ones with me. I have also stopped there to remind myself that any little ache or pain I may have is nothing compared to what she must have endured, and it helps to put things in perspective. Stopping at the location of her cross is kind of like going to the cemetery—it's an attempt to feel closer to her. While her body may be at the cemetery, I know Stormi isn't at either place; she's in heaven. The pain of losing a child is the worst pain there is; you *have* to find comfort in something. For me, occasionally stopping at her cross and sharing a story, a laugh, or a tear with her helps me feel just a little closer.

Obviously, I don't look at "memorial crosses" the same way I used to and never will again. I suppose having one out there that's for one of your own children will do that to you. Now, every cross I drive past causes me to think about the person who died there and the lives that were affected. I guess when it comes right down to it, that's why it's there, to get us thinking. It's there to remind us of a life lost. It reminds us that while possibly only one person physically died there, many people died there emotionally. It's there as a reminder . . . a remembrance . . . a memorial . . .

Having her cross there does not erase my pain of losing Stormi. Nothing can or will ever do that. But it's comforting for me to know that others may drive past, see the name STORMI, and offer up a little prayer. They may have known her and remember some of the good times they had together. They may shed a tear, they may crack a smile, they may do both. I know I have. They may have never heard of someone named Stormi and wonder who she was and what had happened there. Either way, Stormi will never be forgotten, at least partially because of a cross in the ditch . . .

Anticipation. Anticipation in reverse. Have you ever had something you didn't want to do but knew you had to? And you knew that "something" was going to be the hardest thing you had ever done? That "something" for me was Stormi's visitation. As much as I didn't want the visitation time to arrive because I knew how hard it would be, I wanted it because I hoped I would somehow find comfort there. I know that sounds strange, but I don't know how else to explain the time leading up to Stormi's visitation. Tuesday was coming whether I wanted it to or not. I knew the visitation for one of my own children would be the hardest thing I had ever done—that is, until the funeral service for one of my own children the following day. I didn't know if finding comfort at a visitation was possible, but I sure was hopeful because anything was better than the way I was feeling.

The time span between making the arrangements and the actual visitation seemed to drag on forever, yet the visitation was there in a flash. I hadn't been much more than a walking zombie since the pager had gone off on Saturday morning. I knew I had to somehow pull myself together. How do you prepare for something like that? I didn't know what to expect, didn't know what to say to people. How was I going to react to seeing my daughter in her coffin? I kept replaying the scene in my head from just four days before when I watched Stormi walk out to her car after Thanksgiving dinner. Thanksgiving . . . from now on it was going to be the day before Stormi died.

Stormi's family gathered at the funeral home before the visitation start time to have some private time together with each other and with her. We met in the lobby with a member of the funeral home staff. There were a lot of hugs and tears while standing there—and the day was just getting started. I was scared beyond scared to walk through the doors into the large room where Stormi was. As we waited for everyone to arrive, some flowers were delivered, purple ones. Imagine that, something purple for Stormi. Somehow that made it just a little easier to walk into the room where Stormi was.

Walking through those doors was almost a déjà vu thing. We had just done the same thing seven and a half weeks before for Ma Sue. I knew all too well how the room was laid out. I knew where the kitchenette was and where the refreshments would be served, where the DVD that had been put together of Stormi's life would be playing, which walls would have picture collages of Stormi and flower arrangements by them, I knew right where Stormi would be. While there was a moment of déjà vu walking into the room, it quickly went away. The loss of Ma Sue was very painful, but this was a different kind of pain. As I said before, you expect that at some point in time you will be burying your parents and maybe your spouse, but not one of your children. One other *huge* difference . . . with Ma Sue, Stormi was there mourning with the rest of us, and now *she* was the reason we were there. We were mourning *for* her instead of *with* her.

I couldn't believe my eyes when we walked into the room. Other than in a greenhouse, I don't think I have ever seen so many flower arrangements and plants in one place. The room actually smelled of flowers. There were picture collages, there were some of Stormi's collectable items, there was the football signed by Matt Birk that she never got to see, there were so many things it was overwhelming. And at the far end of the room was Stormi Liz. Because of the distance from her, and even with my height of almost six feet, two inches, I could only see some of her hair and a little of her forehead. I wanted to run. I just wasn't sure if I wanted to run to her or for the door.

Never in my worst nightmares did I ever imagine I would be walking toward one of my children lying in a casket. I can honestly say it was the longest walk of my life. I looked at some of the flowers with the nametags on them and the collages on my way to seeing Stormi. I'm not sure if I was really looking at them or if I was just stalling.

And then, there I was, looking at Stormi. There is *no* way to describe the feeling of standing in front of your child in her casket. My knees got week. I shook, I cried, I called out her name.

It's going to sound like a cliché, but she looked peaceful. Jamie and Bonny had done a great job picking out clothes for Stormi. Just like me, Stormi was perfectly happy wearing jeans. She is wearing the same jeans, shirt, and jean jacket she wore for some of her senior pictures. She looked beautiful. The little scrape on her nose was barely noticeable. I think those who didn't know about it ahead of time didn't even know it was there. In her hands was the pendant she had received only weeks before. The story behind that pendant alone was almost enough to make me drop to my knees.

In flashback after flashback I replayed her life. "Flash forward" after "flash forward" I envisioned what could have/should have been. It's going to sound strange, but standing there looking at her reminded me of the hundreds of times I stood next to the crib when the girls were babies. They would be crying and I would scoop them up and try to make it all better. This time I was the one crying . . . who was going to scoop me up? Who was going to make any of this better? It was time to give other family members a chance to spend time with her. I touched her hand; it felt *so* cold. I gave her her favorite "Daddy kiss," the one on the forehead, and told her I loved her. It wasn't easy to walk away, but I headed down the line to look at more flowers and pictures.

It was now time for everyone to gather around the projection screen and watch the DVD of Stormi's life. There weren't enough chairs for everyone to sit, but I made sure I got one. I figured I was going to be standing for the next several hours greeting people, so I might as well sit while I could. Also, I was still thinking about how weak my knees felt when I was standing next to Stormi. I didn't think watching the DVD would be much easier . . . and it wasn't. Just as we had done for Ma Sue, we had gone through books and boxes of pictures and gave them to the staff of the funeral home. They put the pictures on a DVD set to music. In Stormi's case, there were four of her favorite songs. The DVD did just what it was supposed to, it took us through Stormi's life. There were pictures of her from infancy through the week before her death. There were pictures of her by herself, with family, and with friends. Some of the pictures I hadn't seen for a long time and a few I had never seen. The very last picture was one of Stormi and me sitting on the ground together at a concert earlier that summer. It's the last picture I have of the two of us together, and you can't imagine how much that picture means to me. It was very difficult to watch of course, but there were a few pictures that made me smile and even come close to laughing. Laughing . . . there's something I didn't know if and when would happen again. Stormi couldn't laugh, so why should I? How could I laugh without feeling guilty? Why would I want to laugh again? My mind was as big a mess as my heart was. The DVD wasn't even done playing, it wasn't even time for the actual visitation to start, but people were starting to arrive. Ready or not, here we go . . .

It didn't take long before there was a line of people, a long line. I stood as close to Stormi as I could, but I had to leave room for other people to stand by her to pay their respects, and like I said, there were a lot of flowers along the way. Jamie and Bonny were close to Stormi as well. As I said before, Jamie and Stormi considered themselves "better than best friends." It was difficult to see Jamie so heartbroken. She had lost her sister and her best friend at the same time. Besides grieving for Stormi, I knew I had to give Jamie some extra love. I know that sounds like common sense, but it's very easy to get so wrapped up in your own grief and all that needs to be done that you forget about the needs and pain of those around you. I also looked at Bonny and saw the pain on her face. Just because we were divorced didn't change the fact that we'd had two children together. She had lost her child just as I had lost mine. My heart ached for her too.

As people came through the line, I greeted each one with a hug and a request to please wear their seatbelts. It didn't matter how old, how young, or if I knew them or not, they all received at least those two things. As people greeted me they probably noticed something: those purple Vikings sweatpants. I held on to them for dear life. That may have raised an eyebrow or two, but I didn't care, it was what I needed to do to survive at that moment. I needed that connection to Stormi.

I could see the line continuing to get longer. We weren't coming even close to keeping up to the number of people coming in the door. The line was actually starting to weave back and forth in the lobby. Eventually someone I was greeting told me that the line was now outside. I felt bad for those people; it was every bit as cold outside that night as it was the night of the accident. I didn't know what to do, I didn't want to rush people, but I didn't want people standing outside in the freezing cold either.

Stormi's relatives were there of course, as well as friends and high school classmates. Her graduating class had sent flowers. It was hard to see them so sad. I think at that age they think they're invincible. It had been thrown in their faces that isn't the case and it was hard for them to accept losing a friend. Teachers, principals, so many people I never expected to see—but then again, I didn't know what to expect.

There were people I expected to see and they were there. One was a couple from Woodville that I had known for years. He was a member of the fire department and had been an EMT at one time. Besides being from the same town and working together with fire/EMS, we had one other thing in common. They had buried a son because of a car accident. Their son had been a young man in his twenties with a wife and children. I knew they would be there. I had seen them in line, and I knew what was going to happen when they reached me. I had held up pretty well to that point, but I lost it then, and they lost it—we lost it together.

There were a *lot* of people I didn't know and I made sure I asked every one of them who they were and how they knew Stormi. I was pleasantly shocked by some of their answers. I expected that I would see Stormi's bosses and some of her coworkers, but I didn't expect that I would meet some of the customers that she served food to. And it wasn't just one or two people. There were a lot who said they knew her from where she worked. They weren't just from the Hammond Hotel either, which was only three miles from Baldwin, they were there from Ciatti's in Woodbury which was almost forty-five minutes away. That just blew me away, that people who only knew her from where she worked would come to pay their respects. And it's not like they knew her from spending extended periods of time together. She took their food order and later brought it to them. That to me was a *huge* honor, that she made that big an impression on people she barley knew.

It was amazing how many people where there; I couldn't believe it. At one point the funeral home staff had to print more of the bulletins that had Stormi's obituary in it because they ran out. They later told me they estimated there were fifteen hundred people that went through the reception line. That's more people than live in some small towns. I couldn't believe it. By the time Sandy my ambulance director got to talk to me, she had stood in line for two and a half hours. That was amazing to me on two levels; first, that people were willing to do that in-spite of the bitter cold because some of that time was spent standing outside, and second, Stormi was only eighteen. I could only be that lucky to have that many friends and have made that big an impression on people that they were willing to do that. What an honor.

People said many wonderful things about Stormi. It was nice to hear how she had touched their lives. There were some people who had never met Stormi but knew Jamie, Bonny, or me. The EMTs and rescue people who had given it their all for Stormi were there. Some of them looked like they had been crying as much as I had. Being an EMT can be *very* rewarding, but being an EMT can downright *suck* sometimes. Even one of the doctors who attended to Stormi in the emergency room in Baldwin was there with his wife. She had worked with Stormi at the Hammond Hotel. More tears.

The visitation went well more than an hour longer than the scheduled time. During that time, I never left my "post," not even to use the restroom. I never went any further than to Stormi to touch her hand for a second or two, and then right back to the reception line I went. Bonny and Jamie were never far away either. There was always someone kind enough to bring me a bite to eat or something to drink. No one bothered to ask me if I wanted to sit down; they knew it wouldn't have done any good, no way was I sitting.

I was deeply honored and touched by the number of people there and the wonderful things they said. There were plenty of tears and even a few smiles with the things people said. But there was a mother and her daughter who had the story that put the "icing on the cake." I had never seen them before, have never seen them since. I remember that the daughter was maybe in her mid-teens, the mom was probably fortyish. I couldn't possibly tell you what they looked like and it doesn't matter; what does matter is what they said. When I asked them the "how do you know Stormi" question, here's what they said: they were recently new to Hammond. They had moved to town without knowing a single person. One evening they decided to go out for a bite to eat and ended up at the Hammond Hotel where Stormi was their server. They said the atmosphere was okay, the food was okay, but Stormi was perfect. She treated them like they had always lived in town right next door to her. They said they had a wonderful time with her that evening. They also said they went back to the Hammond Hotel that same evening each week so Stormi would be their server. They said they went so they could see her and her happy-go-lucky personality, her light-up-the-room smile, and because she treated them like she had always known them. After hearing that I lost it—no, "came unglued" is probably more accurate. I don't think I was ever more proud of Stormi than at that moment.

I think it goes to show that as life goes on, we don't always know whom we're going to impress, we don't always know how or when we're going to impress someone. We may never even know the whos, hows, or whens of the impressions we have made because they may be reveled beyond our lifetime. Hopefully we have impressed people in a positive way . . . I guess the lesson learned is to treat people as if I have always known them and as if I may never see them again.

The people were finally gone and it was time to leave. I stood by Stormi for a while again. I still couldn't believe it was real, that this was really happening. I touched her hand, gave her her "Daddy kiss," told her how proud I was of her, told her how much I loved her, and told her I would see her the next day. The last part may sound like a strange thing to say to your child lying in casket, but I guess I don't ever remember anyone telling me what the right thing to say is. Truth of it was, I knew when I saw her the next day it would be the last time I *ever* saw her. As hard as it was to walk into that room, it was even harder to walk out. I didn't want to leave her. As I was walking out, I thought about how the afternoon and evening had gone. All things considered, I thought it went pretty well, and I hoped that the next day did the same.

I had found comfort in numbers. I had found comfort in the things people said. I had found comfort . . .

Anticipation. Anticipation in reverse. Isn't it kind of ironic that the first four letters of the word anticipation are "anti"?

I woke the morning of Stormi's funeral not knowing what to expect from the day. It wasn't, of course, a very good night's sleep I was waking up from, but I suppose that's understandable. I had clutched those Vikings sweatpants while trying to fall asleep after getting home from the visitation just as I had done every night since the accident. I made sure they were ready to take with me to her funeral.

As I was getting up and getting myself going, I "rehearsed" Stormi's eulogy in my head. I had jotted down a few notes of what I wanted to say and what her mom wanted me to say, but 99 percent of her eulogy was in my head. I had studied forensics in high school, and even though there had been a lot of years between then and 2005, I was used to writing speeches on short notice and speaking in front of people. I had no idea at the time of course how valuable that experience would be, not only at the time of Ma Sue and Stormi's funerals but later on when I started going to high schools and talking to kids about Stormi's accident. In any event, I wanted her eulogy to be perfect. I couldn't get it out of my head that Stormi's visitation and funeral needed to be every bit as special as her birth and life had been. It would be a much different kind of special, of course, but I wanted it to be something Stormi would be proud of, just as I was proud of her.

I had to pick up my funeral suit from the drycleaners that morning. I call it a funeral suit because that's what I bought it for, and funerals are the only time I wear it. "Suits" and I don't like each other very much. I told the girls' mom when we were together, I have told my family, and I told my fiancée: don't bury me in a suit when my time comes because I prefer the casual look of jeans. Stormi was the same way; casual suited her just fine. I also picked up a Minnesota Vikings pennant on the way back home. It's the one that's buried with her.

Stormi's visitation continued at the church for one hour prior to her funeral service starting. We arrived well ahead of time and there were already people there. Just as had happened the previous afternoon at the funeral home, it didn't take long before the church was full of people. Once again I was overwhelmed by the number of people who were there for Stormi Liz, and I was deeply honored. Some of the people I remembered seeing at the visitation and some not. I couldn't believe there were yet still more people coming to pay their respects.

The O'Connell Funeral Home "family" had done a wonderful job helping our family with Ma Sue's visitation and funeral, and that level of help and compassion more then continued with Stormi's. When we arrived at the church, it looked much like the funeral home had, like a greenhouse. It must have taken several trips to move all of the picture colleges, plants, flower arrangements, and memorabilia from the funeral home, but it was all there. Again I was amazed by the amount of "stuff" that had been pulled together in such a short period of time. The back of the sanctuary where the visitation was continuing is much smaller than the funeral home, so some of the plants and flowers had to be kept in an office until after the service was complete.

The visitation at the church didn't have an organized "receiving line" of people like it did at the funeral home. Some people "viewed" Stormi and paid their respects, some people stopped and talked to her family, and some went directly to the church pews and waited for the funeral service to start. Because of the lack of space, I stood a little farther away from Stormi than I had the day before. I wanted to make sure that anyone who wanted to view Stormi had the opportunity to do so. As I stood there holding on to those sweatpants for dear life, I was still in total disbelief over what was happening. How could this have happened, why did this happen, when was the pain going to go away? Lots of questions and no answers.

There is no way any parent should ever have to stand there waiting for the funeral service for one of his children to start. Just because I wanted it to be a special and meaningful service didn't mean I was in any hurry for it to start. And yet because it hadn't started, standing there was pure hell. It was a mixed bag of many emotions; I didn't want the funeral to ever start, I wanted it to be so special that it would never be finished, and yet I wanted it to be done and to be as far away from that building as possible. I didn't want to have to bury one of my children but had no choice. I wanted her service to be the most special one ever but didn't ever want it to take place. On top of all that I was standing in a church, in "God's house," and I had serious questions whether God knew what He was doing. It bothered me that God had "allowed" this to happen.

It bothered me that I was questioning God; that's not the way I was raised to think. There were so many thoughts in my head that made perfect sense, and at the same time made no sense at all. But no matter what I did or didn't think, no matter what I did or didn't feel, there was no avoiding the fact that there was going to be a funeral for Stormi. I had known that since I had lifted her eyelids in the emergency room at the hospital.

Way too soon yet not nearly soon enough, it was time for the funeral to start, the funeral for an eighteen-year-old, the funeral for one of my children, Stormi's funeral. The funeral home directors asked Stormi's family and pallbearers to head for a private room in the church basement. They wanted to explain to everyone how the service was going to be conducted, where the family was to sit, the duties of the pallbearers, and to gather for a brief prayer.

By this time most of Stormi's family had said their goodbyes to her, and they headed straight for the basement. Her immediate family took a few more moments to say their final goodbyes. I can still see the pain on Dad's face and in his eyes. It was a repeat of the heartbreak I had seen on his face just eight weeks before when he'd buried his wife of forty-seven years, and now he was standing in front of a coffin that was holding his granddaughter of eighteen years. The scene of one of my daughters having to say a final goodbye to my other daughter is one I will never be able to forget. It was a scene that cut deep, all the way to down to my soul. It was a different kind of love, but I know the girls shared a love for each other that could rival the love a parent feels for his child. Jamie was left with a hole in her heart that was as big as the one in mine.

Bonny and I arrived alongside Stormi at the same time. Bonny politely but firmly told me she had brought Stormi into the world and she would be the last one to see her leave. It didn't really seem like the time or place for a disagreement, but I didn't have a valid argument against that statement anyway. I loved my daughters as much as any dad could, but I don't know that any man can ever fully understand the bond a woman has with her child; conception, womb development, birth, newborn care. It just seems to me that except for the "fifteen minutes of fame" that is a father's part in the process of giving life to a child, men are always trying to catch up to the same feeling of closeness a mother has with a child. I told Bonny that was just fine and I walked up to Stormi.

There are no words that can describe the feelings I had standing there in front of Stormi. There are no words that can describe the feelings I had knowing it would be the last time I would see her . . . *ever*. Knowing I will see her again in heaven someday was doing nothing for me at that moment. If I had died and gone to heaven that very moment it wouldn't have been soon enough, and it had already been five days since I had last seen or talked to her. I didn't want to wait to see her again in heaven someday, I wanted her to be among the walking and talking. But that wasn't reality. Reality was that she was lying in a coffin in front of me, reality was that I wasn't ever going to see her again. The feelings of "I don't ever want to leave" and "get me out here" were hitting me at the same time again. I didn't know what to do, didn't know what to say. I felt as helpless as a newborn. So many thoughts, and yet there was nothing moving in my brain. For half a second I thought about leaving the Vikings sweatpants in the coffin with her next to the pennant. The selfish part of me kicked in and I decided I needed them worse than she did. I rationalized that she would have agreed. I noticed there was a little piece of paper sticking out of the drawer that held the letters that had been written for Stormi to take to heaven with her. I opened the drawer to tuck the piece of paper back in and was amazed at how many letters there were. Knowing Stormi had a family and so many friends who loved her so much helped break me out of my inability to think, or to not do anything but stand there. I touched Stormi's hand and the pendant that had meant so much to her. I told her how much I loved her and how proud I was of her, gave her her "Daddy kiss," and moved out of the way so her mom could say goodbye. I wasn't ready to go directly to the basement, but I didn't want to stand there and watch Bonny say goodbye either. She deserved her private time with Stormi—and I didn't need to witness anymore heartbreak.

The time spent in the basement was brief, with instructions being given and a short prayer offered by one of the pastors. Understandably, the walk back up to the sanctuary seemed to be a million times longer than the walk to the basement had been. When we got to the top of the stairs, I noticed right away that the coffin holding Stormi had been moved to the front of the sanctuary. The walk down the center aisle of the church wasn't a "short walk" either. Because I had "tunnel vision" and was focused on Stormi's coffin up ahead of me, I didn't see people other than those sitting on the ends of the pews. I had no idea at that time just how many people were in the sanctuary, but that would be changing soon enough. Stormi's family was seated in the front rows of pews that had been reserved for them on the right-hand side of the church. Her immediate family was seated in the very front rows, with extended family behind them. I sat in the front row, only a couple of feet from where I had sat with Jamie on one side of me and STORMI on the other at Ma Sue's funeral just eight weeks earlier. Ready or not, it was time for the funeral to start. *Never want to leave, but get me out of here!*

The man who was the church pastor and who'd performed Ma Sue's service had some opening remarks and an opening prayer. It was then time for Sharon to sing her the first song, "There's Holes in the Floor of Heaven." It wasn't a song I was familiar with, but Sharon sang it so well that it didn't matter if I knew it or not. Besides that, Sharon wasn't singing it for me, she was singing it for Stormi because Stormi enjoyed country music and that song. As soon as Sharon was done singing, it was my turn to do something for Stormi. It was time for me to give her eulogy.

I can't say I was at all nervous walking up the steps to the pulpit to give Stormi's eulogy. I knew what I wanted to say and knew how I wanted it to go, so I felt prepared. There was one thing I wasn't quite prepared for, though. I wasn't expecting to see the amount of people I saw, not even close. I had been so focused on getting to the front of the sanctuary that I had walked past all kinds of people who were standing because there wasn't even enough room for everyone to sit! The balcony was full, the two rooms behind the balcony were full, and the overflow area behind the sanctuary was full. Once again I was deeply honored by the number of people who were there for Stormi Liz.

I started Stormi's eulogy in the same manner I had started Ma Sue's, by reading her obituary. I'm not sure why I started them that way, but it's what I did. I then started talking about Stormi. Using a couple of serious stories, I talked about how she was as unique as her name; I told people about how Stormi had rearranged her college class schedules after Ma Sue passed away just so she was available on Thursdays to go to the mission with Dad, and I told about how when she was little she would tell her mom, "I love you 100,045" because it was the biggest number she could think of. Using a number of humorous stories, I talked about how she was as unique as her name was; I talked about how her attitude could sometimes be as "stormy" as her name, I talked about how she had her own detention chair at school because she was always late, I talked about her cell phone getting taken away by the principal, I told everyone attending her funeral how Stormi had told the family on Thanksgiving Day why she and I looked like each other, and I talked about the concert tickets she had won at the Minnesota State Fair. The ticket story goes like this: a local radio station was having a contest at the fair, with the winner taking home tickets to an Usher concert. The contestant who did the most "wild and crazy" thing was declared the winner, and that was a contest right up Stormi's alley. Stormi had walked over to the horse barn, collected a bunch of "horse apples," and then smeared the "apples" all over herself in front of the radio station's stand. She smeared them on her skin, on her clothes, and in her hair. Needless to say Stormi was declared the winner.

I made sure there were more humorous stories than serious ones for a couple of reasons. First, not long after I was done with her eulogy, the pastor would be starting on the sermon, or message, for Stormi's funeral service. I wanted people to be at ease when he started talking and not all tense. His job was hard enough because he had to somehow convince the people in the sanctuary that it was somehow "okay" that an eighteen-year-old was lying in the now-sealed coffin in front of the pulpit. Count me among those who needed convincing. Also, while we were obviously there mourning the loss of Stormi, we were also there to celebrate her life. The best way I could think of to do that was to tell "Stormi stories" that demonstrated just how full of life and attitude she had been.

Next, for the first time in my life, I talked publically about my out-of-body-experience. Mom, Dad, Jamie, Stormi, and other immediate family members had known about it, but I had never talked about it in front of a large group. I guess prior to that I didn't feel it was something I needed to "broadcast." Now I felt it was necessary to tell everyone in that sanctuary, and then some, about it. I wanted the world to know that if I felt the incredible sense of peace, calm, and security I had just from "being near" a crucifix on a wall, imagine how good Stormi and Ma Sue feel being in the presence of God himself in heaven. I wanted people to know that Stormi wasn't cold, scared, in pain—wasn't anything anymore but happy. I don't know if it made anyone else feel better, but it made me feel a tremendous amount better knowing that.

I also explained to everyone why I was standing at the pulpit holding a pair of Vikings sweatpants. I explained why they had also seen me holding them the day before at her visitation. I simply said I was holding them because I had to. Because I couldn't hold Stormi, I had to hold something that made me feel close to her. I said that because she was such a huge Vikings fan, I couldn't think of anything else of hers that could make me feel the same closeness those sweatpants did. I imagine there were a few people who thought I had "gone off the deep end." Call me selfish, but I didn't care what they thought, I cared what I felt.

I finished by thanking everyone for their love and support. I said there was no way Stormi's family could have gotten through the days since her accident without that love and support. The number of people attending the visitation and the number of people even *standing* through her funeral service were evidence of that love and support. I also asked that everyone please buckle their seatbelts each and every time they got in their vehicles. I asked the young people there to please call their parents for a ride home if they had had even one drink. I closed by thanking God for letting us "borrow" Stormi for eighteen years, adding that I wished we would have had her much longer.

It was the pastor of Bonny's church's turn to try and make some sense of the day, out of the past five days. Just as you couldn't give me the job of chaplain at a hospital, you couldn't give me the job of being the pastor who has to deliver a funeral message for a young person, for my daughter. And again, just as the chaplain at the hospital had had his work cut out for him, so did this pastor. I didn't know what to expect, I didn't know what to think. I knew it wasn't the chaplain's fault Stormi had died, and I knew it wasn't the pastor's fault, and deep down I even knew it wasn't God's fault, yet

I thought one of the three should have been able to give me some answers as to *why* she'd died . . . I was still waiting.

As I sat there I thought about Jamie and Stormi sitting on each side of me during Ma Sue's funeral. I recalled how Stormi and I had gotten a chuckle out of one of Ma Sue's flower arrangements catching on fire toward the end of her service due to an overzealous candle. We had watched the fire closely and I was able to wait until the pastor was done with his message before getting up and putting the fire out. It had added a light moment to the heaviness of Ma Sue's funeral.

Now I was looking for a light moment, I was looking for answers, I was looking at Stormi's coffin, I was looking for a way out of the whole situation. *Never leave, get me out of here* . . . this pastor had his work cut out for him.

The first thing the pastor did was to ask people to slide a little closer to each other in the pews so that those who were standing had a chance to sit. I heard some shuffling behind me, but I didn't turn around to see the results. He then opened by saying that while Stormi had been confirmed in and for the most part attended the same church I did, he did have the privilege of meeting Stormi on a number of occasions. He said Stormi had even spent the night at his house because she was a classmate of his daughter. He said he found her to be a "respectful and delightful" young lady. That brought a bit of a smile to my face and to my heart. Yet another person had something nice to say about Stormi. I know people typically say positive things about someone who has passed, but this wasn't just any "someone," this was my daughter. As far as making me feel a little better goes, the pastor seemed to be off on the right foot.

Then came his message. I don't remember how long he talked, and I by no means remember his exact verbiage, but I clearly remember the gist of his message, which was that Stormi was now a "newborn" again and was just starting her "life," and those of us still on Earth are the ones who are slowly but surely dying. His message was that we could take comfort in knowing that she now gets to live forever in heaven. His message was that with the wonderful life Stormi now enjoys, there would be no reason she would want to come back from heaven.

Was his message an overly simplistic one? Maybe. Would his message work for everyone? Maybe not. Did his message work for me? Absolutely. No one will ever be able to fully satisfy my question of "why"—not the chaplain, not the pastor, not even God. I knew the pain of losing Stormi wasn't going to go away because of something the pastor or anyone said. I knew because of my own experience that Stormi was just fine in heaven. I knew she was now going to "live" forever. I knew that we on Earth are all going to die someday. What he did say that worked for me was that Stormi is now a "newborn" again. I thought back to how helpless she was a newborn. I thought back to my middle-of-the-night rocking chair sessions with her. I then thought about Stormi sitting on God's lap in a big ole rocking chair in heaven, safe, content, and sleeping, just like she had been on my lap. I had what I needed. The pastor had done his job and then some.

With the pastor's message complete, it was time for Sharon to sing again. I don't know if this was the moment I was most looking forward to, or if it was the one I was dreading the most. It was time for Sharon to sing "Jesus Loves Me." The same song, sung the same way, by the same person who had sung at Stormi's baptism. Even as I write this, I can still hear it being sung at her baptism. I can still see the pastor walk up the steps from the baptismal fount to the pulpit and then hold little Stormi in the air so the whole congregation could see her. Even as I write this, I can still hear it being sung at her funeral. Only now Stormi was lying in a coffin in front of that same pulpit. The baptismal fount was fewer than ten feet in front and to the right of me.

Before she started to sing, Sharon announced that she had sung "Jesus Loves Me" for Stormi's baptism and was honored to sing it for her again. I felt that was a very thoughtful thing for her to do, and it added so much meaning to the moment. To say Sharon sang the song beautifully would be a huge understatement. It was every bit as beautiful as it had been at Stormi's baptism. And when it comes right down to it, I think it was even more meaningful. The words, the meaning behind the words, the reason we were there, the beauty with which it was sung, it all added up to the song being a real "tearjerker." As if my tears needed any jerking. They were flowing just fine without any help. I couldn't see behind me of course, but I can't imagine there were many other dry eyes either. Had there been any life in those Vikings sweatpants, I would have squeezed it right out of them for holding on to them so tight at that point . . . they also came in handy once again for "dabbing away" my tears. I can honestly think of no better way to have Stormi's funeral come to a close than with that song. I can honestly think of no one who could have brought the meaning and feeling to it that Sharon did. Stormi's funeral was now almost finished. The part of me that wanted the funeral to be done and over with and to get away from that place was about to be satisfied. The part of me that wanted the funeral to never end and to never leave there was about to be disappointed. I still didn't have a clue as to what I was thinking.

The first pastor had a few closing announcements before his closing prayer. He announced that we would be heading to the cemetery for internment, and that anyone who wanted to attend the committal was welcome to do so. He added that there would be a luncheon in the basement reception hall of the church after the committal was finished. Again, anyone who wanted to attend was welcome to do so. He then closed with a prayer. And just like that, the funeral for one of my children, Stormi's funeral, was complete.

The funeral directors moved Stormi's coffin away from the pulpit to the beginning of the center aisle. Her pallbearers then moved alongside Stormi and started the long walk to the hearse waiting outside. I and the rest of Stormi's immediate family were right behind them. I noticed that while there were fewer people still standing, there were a few who had stood for the entire service. Row by row the funeral home directors dismissed the rest of the people in attendance, and everyone headed for their vehicles so they could go to the cemetery.

The scenes of Stormi's coffin being loaded into the hearse at the church and then unloaded at the cemetery will be ingrained in my memory for the rest of my life. I can still see the tremendously long line of cars in the procession headed to the cemetery. I can still see the flashing lights of the police cars as they stopped traffic at intersections so we could pass through. I can still see the look of sorrow in the eyes of one of the officers when our eyes met as he was standing outside his police car at one of the intersections. He was the officer who had pulled me over while I was trying to "catch"

Stormi when she was meeting friends for lunch instead of being at school where she was supposed to be. I can still feel the bitter cold as we walked to Stormi's gravesite. I can still feel the feeling of wanting to run, the same way I felt it the day before at the start of her visitation. Once again, I wasn't sure if I wanted to run to her or for the door . . . any door.

Other then the initial shock of losing her sister, I think the committal was probably the hardest time of all for Jamie. I have no idea what thoughts were going through her mind at that time, but I could easily see the pain on her face and hear it in her sobs.

There were five or six chairs set up for the immediate family, and the rest stood. With as many people as I saw gathered around, I can't imagine there were many who stayed at the church. The pastor who had given the message for the funeral service offered a brief prayer. I then said a few words, and then everyone just stood there. It was so cold that I thought everyone would have left right away, but they didn't, they just stood there. I don't think anyone else wanted to leave Stormi any more then I did.

The fact that it was so bitterly cold must have been heavy on Jamie's mind. She stood up from her chair, took off her coat, and laid it on the coffin holding her best friend and sister. It was a gesture of love that brought tears to my and many other peoples' eyes. I tried to get her to put it back on, but she refused. I took my coat off and draped it over her shoulders, but she didn't want that either. We stood there for the next few minutes with both of our coats keeping Stormi warm. Eventually we put our coats back on and I invited anyone who wanted to to take a flower with them from the large arrangement that had been placed on Stormi's coffin. I took two and laid one of them by Ma Sue.

Just as had happened at the hospital when leaving the bereavement room, just as had happened when leaving the visitation the night before, I found it every bit as hard to leave the cemetery as it had been to walk into it. The last time seeing her coffin was a different kind of hard than the last time seeing Stormi, but it was by no means an easy thing to do. I walked to the car feeling like I had just left half my hopes and dreams for the future in the hands of someone else . . . to be placed in the ground after I drove away. The day was getting closer to being done. I was still struggling with the inner battle of trying to decide whether I wanted it to be done or not, whether I wanted to be there or not.

It didn't take long, and the reception hall in the church basement was full of people. The ladies' organizations of the church had worked hard to prepare and serve a wonderful meal. Normally they prepare all the food themselves, but they had help in this instance. Ciatti's, one of Stormi's employers, had worked with the ladies and sent over a good portion of the food. Their generosity was greatly appreciated. To this day, it amazes me the number of lives Stormi touched both far and wide. It's a huge honor as a parent to know your child had that kind of a positive impact on people. Fewer than four years later I would be experiencing the same feeling again because of Jamie.

I talked with as many people as I could during the luncheon. There was no way to get to everyone, but I did my best. There were a lot of hugs and even some more tears. I heard more than one person say, "Your family has been through so much lately; how much more can you take?" I was wondering the same thing but certainly didn't want to know the answer.

Little by little, people started to leave. It occurred to me that still upstairs in the sanctuary were all of the flowers, plants, and memorabilia that had been given and collected for Stormi. Plus there were some more plants in the church office. I already had some plants at home from Ma Sue's funeral. I certainly wanted some of Stormi's but didn't need all of them. The thought occurred to me that her pallbearers would probably appreciate receiving one their friend Stormi's arrangements. I quickly found the pallbearers and gave them all flowers before they left. A couple of arrangements were left in the sanctuary for the next Sunday's service, and the rest of the plants and flowers got divided up between family members. I brought one plant to the Baldwin Hospital where they had tried so hard to save the life of my daughter. As of 2012, that plant continues to do well and has bloomed in late November or early December five of the six years since Stormi's passing, just as it was blooming at the time of her funeral. It's wonderfully taken care of by the staff there.

With all the plants, flowers, and memorabilia dispersed or loaded up, with the ladies who had worked so hard to feed everyone and then clean up afterward now gone, with all the people who had graciously come to pay their respects to their dear family member or friend also gone, there I stood. As I stood there, I was reminded of something that happened when I was in the third grade. It happened when our family had gone to Iowa for the funeral of Grandpa Hielkema, Dad's dad. I don't remember his visitation or his funeral, but I do remember when it was time to leave. I remember the look on Grandma's face. Our family was the last to leave. Dad's siblings and their families had already left, so it was just us and Grandma. I can remember Grandma standing there waving goodbye to us as we were backing out of the driveway. I can remember the look on her face. She had just buried her husband, and then one by one her children and grandchildren had left to go back to their homes in other states. And now the last ones were backing out of the driveway. Reality was setting in with just how alone she was going to be. I will never forget the look on Grandma's face . . . that must have been the same look I had on my face as I stood in the back of that now *empty* sanctuary.

And then it was done, the funeral for one of my children, Stormi's funeral. Whether I wanted to leave or not, it was time . . . all too soon, and not nearly soon enough.

*   *   *

The state patrol does an investigation whenever there is a fatal car crash. Stormi's accident, at least the accident scene part, was investigated the day after the crash. It's necessary to get the investigation done right away so all evidence is undisturbed, especially in the winter. Any new snow could cover up important details. The rest of the investigation continued after the autopsy report was complete and it was known just what her injuries had been. It's incredible how accurate their investigation was.

By using the pitch or angle of the ditch that approaches the crossroad she hit, and the distance her car went through the air, they were able to calculate a range of speed that her car had been traveling. Their calculations gave a range of a couple of mph on each side of seventy. They were also able to tell how many times her car had flipped and rolled. That could be determined from the damage to her car and marks it left in the ditch.

A lot was learned about the accident once the state patrol report was complete and presented to us—more than I wanted to know. They could tell from looking at Stormi's car that the driver's door had popped open during the car's final roll. That determination came from the pieces of paper I had seen at the top of her car door that were trapped between the door and the car's body. I guess if I had been thinking clearly when I looked at her car the day of the accident, it would have been obvious to me that there was only one way for those papers to get in there. The fact that the papers were at the *top* of the door was an important clue. If the door had been opened in a normal manner or situation, and paper had fallen out while the door was then being shut, the paper would have been trapped at the bottom of the door. Again, these pieces of paper were at the top of the door. Her door had definitely popped open while the car was rolling and the papers got trapped in there when it slammed shut.

Because the investigation explained the facts of the accident, and then later the autopsy report showed what her injuries had been, we knew that Stormi was crushed between the door and the frame of the car *as it rolled over her*. The autopsy showed that her sternum (breastbone) and back were both broken at the exact same height in her body. That couldn't happen unless she was crushed or pinched between two objects. We know that it happened on the final roll because she was found only eight and a half feet from the car. As the car was rolling, the door popped open for a fraction of a second; Stormi then started to fall out of the car; the car continued rolling, which forced the door to try to close, pinching Stormi; the car rolled on its driver's side with Stormi pinched between the car and the door; the car rolled far enough upright that the door opened, allowing Stormi to fall onto the ground; the momentum of the continuing roll forced the door to slam shut, trapping the papers where Stormi had just been. The car then finished its final roll, landing on its wheels. All of this happened in the blink of an eye. It all adds up to Stormi not just being between the door and the car, similar to when you get a finger in a door—it means she was there *while the car was on top of her*. I can't begin to tell you how that makes me feel knowing that happened to my daughter.

As I said, Stormi's sternum and back were broken at the exact same height. With her sternum being broken, in addition to the other chest trauma that went along with it, there was bleeding into her chest cavity. That bleeding is ultimately what took her life. They said the rate of the bleeding was slowed down by the cold, but eventually her chest cavity had enough blood in it that her lungs and heart couldn't work properly. Storm's heart stopped beating about the same time they were loading her into the ambulance. The autopsy also showed that she had a "brain bleed." The report said that the area of brain bleed was small enough that it didn't have any bearing on her death. The autopsy did not show any other broken bones. It's no wonder I stood next to her in the emergency room trying to understand why they were doing CPR on someone who only had a scrape on her nose and a cut on a pinky finger. All her injuries were on the inside.

I would imagine anyone reading this can understand why those papers trapped in her car door have tormented me since I first learned why they were there. Of course it's not the papers themselves that torment me, it's what happened to Stormi that does. I try not to, but it's something I can't help but think about sometimes. I think anybody would. It hurts to think about one of your children going through that much trauma. I know she couldn't feel it, but it's hard to think about CPR (chest compressions) being performed on her while her sternum was broke. I clearly remember how much my chest hurt from the bull standing on it, and I can't even imagine how much worse hers hurt. There is no way of knowing for certain one way or the other, but I sometimes wonder if Stormi was conscious at all during the better then six and a half hours she laid out in the cold. That in itself torments me, not knowing if she was able to think during that time. If she was able to think, was she sacred? Did she know she was going to die? I have occasionally wondered that if she was actually conscious part of the time, did she call out for help? Out in the rural countryside where she was, and in the middle of the night, no one would have heard her if she had. Also, with her back broken, she wouldn't have been able to move herself even if she was conscious.

It bothers me to no end that while I was lying in a nice *warm bed sleeping*, Stormi was lying face-down in the *cold snow dying*. The feeling a parent has that he "should have been there" is a horrible one. I can completely understand how Dad felt when I was injured. The truth of it is that no parent can be everywhere. No parent can be with his or her child all the time. I used to think it was going to be great once the girls got their driver's licenses so I didn't have to drive them everywhere. Then once they got them, it was time to worry and I wanted them to be "little" again. It was similar to when the girls were toddlers and I wanted them to walk so they didn't have to be carried, and then they walked and got into stuff they weren't supposed to. I wanted them to talk so they could explain what was wrong or what they wanted, and then they said things they weren't supposed to. I wanted them little again so I could protect them more easily, protect them from themselves and from the big, cruel world. It kind of comes down to letting go of your children and letting them grow up and move on in life. Easier said than done of course. Then again, that kind of letting go is nothing in comparison to way we had to let go of Stormi. *No* parent should ever have to do that. What I wouldn't give to have the simple worries like walking and talking back. As a parent, a person always wants his child to be healthy, safe, warm, and happy, not fearful—a million different adjectives, positive adjectives. Unfortunately, it doesn't always work out that way. There are so many things and scenarios to think about surrounding the whole situation of her accident that it would drive me crazy if I let it. I find comfort in my belief that Ma Sue was "sitting" right beside Stormi, keeping her warm, and helping her to not be scared.

The battery was ripped out of Stormi's car by the force of the accident, meaning there were no headlights shining in the ditch for even a second after the crash. Because the ditch was fairly deep in that area, the headlights of passing cars shined over the top of Stormi and her car. That helps explain why she wasn't found until morning once it was light out. That helps explain why other kids who were at the same party she was at drove right past her on their way to their homes. They drove within fifty feet of their friend lying in ditch, lying in a ditch in twelve-degree weather wearing only jeans and two shirts while her chest slowly filled with blood.

There may have been others who drove past Stormi that I am not aware of, but there is one person who I am very aware of. He lives (at least he did at the time of the accident) about twenty-five miles to the southeast and worked about twenty miles to the northwest of where the accident was. Part of his drive to work took him on County Road E, and he drove past Stormi slightly less than two hours before she was found. He wasn't at work very long though, and he ended up seeing Stormi anyway, just in a completely different setting. He was the paramedic/helicopter pilot who flew her from the Baldwin Hospital to Regions. Isn't life full of cruel ironies?

Stormi's car had a "black box" in it. It served the same purpose as the ones airplanes have. It continuously monitored some of the activities of her car and recorded the last five seconds of those activities prior to the crash. It showed that her car was traveling at seventy mph up until the very last second before the crash, and then it went down to sixty-nine mph. You can see what I mean about the accuracy of the state patrol investigation. The posted speed limit on County Road E is fifty-five mph.

The black box showed her seatbelt had not been worn during the five seconds that was recorded. It was confirmation of what we already knew, that she'd been ejected from her car because she wasn't belted in. But it also proved she didn't take the seatbelt off at the last second and try to jump out. Her car was heavily damaged, but for what it went through, you would have thought it would have been worse. Here's my point: had the seatbelt been worn, there's a very good chance Stormi would be alive today. There's no doubt she would have been injured, but she would have stayed in the car instead of being crushed by it. Since her accident, if someone gets in my car and doesn't immediately put his or her seatbelt on, I tell the person that Stormi is "yelling" to put it on.

The black box also showed that her brakes were never applied. At seventy mph, your vehicle travels almost one hundred three feet per second. From the point where her car left her lane of traffic, crossed the opposite lane, entered the ditch, and hit the crossroad, it took about four and a half seconds at seventy mph. That's the total time, four and a half seconds. From that four and a half seconds, you have to take away the amount of time it would have taken for her car to come to a stop—in other words, braking distance. It doesn't do any good to apply your brakes once your car is airborne. That brings her available time to react to the situation down to approximately two seconds. And of course, her reaction time would have been compromised by the fact that she had been drinking. In other words, once she deviated from her lane of traffic, her fate was pretty much sealed.

If only that crossroad hadn't been there . . .

If only she hadn't been drinking . . .

If only she hadn't been using her cell phone . . .

If only she had worn her seatbelt . . .

If only she hadn't been tired . . .

If only you could live on "if only" . . .

*   *   *

I went to the local high school where Stormi graduated from and talked to the students, all four hundred of them, at prom time in April 2006. That was only five months after the accident. I talked to the students about her accident, showed them pictures of her car on the overhead screen, and told them every last detail of the crash and her death. I talked to them about what it was like to lose one of my children. I talked about many things, including wearing seatbelts. In October 2006 there was a car accident involving three teenage girls.

Two of them were students of that same school and were likely in attendance of my talk, the other was a former student. Two of the girls died as a result of the accident, and the third was critically injured.

None had been wearing seatbelts . . .

The weeks and months that followed Stormi's accident and funeral were a struggle. Who am I kidding by saying "weeks and months"? As I write this it's been more than six years and there are still occasional struggles. I have heard many people say after losing a loved one that they wished the world around them would stop so they could catch their breath. That of course doesn't happen. Unless your loved was someone well known or famous, most of the "world" outside your family or immediate area doesn't even know your loved one passed away. It doesn't really seem fair, does it? There were times I wanted to scream at the top of my lungs that Stormi and Ma Sue had died. I wanted the world to know what a wonderful person Stormi had been. I wanted everyone to know how much she would have contributed to the world. I wanted the world to know much I loved her. I wanted the world to share some of my grief. I wanted the world to stop so I could catch my breath—that of course didn't happen.

It didn't take long for me to figure out that indeed the world wasn't going to stop, that the lives of everyone around me kept going, and mine needed to also. Besides the normal routine of life that had to continue, there were now extra "things" to do, things that were the direct result of Stormi being gone. My construction business still needed to be managed, plus now there were final details of Stormi's personal belongings and loans to be handled, Jamie needed some extra attention, and there was grief to deal with.

Keeping my mind on work wasn't an easy thing to do, but I had employees who depended on me to keep them working. I knew and worked with a lot of people in the construction industry, and just as happened when I would bump into someone I knew in everyday life, I was always greeted with a handshake, hug, or an "I'm sorry" by my counterparts in the construction industry. Their compassion, as well as everyone else's along the way, greatly helped my badly broken heart.

Car insurance paid off the lease company on Stormi's new car that she'd been so proud of. She had a couple of small balances on credit cards from department stores, and those balances were "forgiven" by the credit card companies. The college Stormi was attending sent a check for her full tuition amount before there was even a discussion about it. That was something that was really appreciated because the check, and gifts of money received in cards, was used to help defray the cost of her funeral. Every time something needed to be resolved, it was like rubbing salt in an open wound, having to explain to someone on the phone or in person what had happened. It wasn't done right away, but eventually her personal items were gone and decisions were made as to what to do with them.

I took about a month off of my EMT duties after Stormi's accident. I was offered more time off, but I knew I had to get back into the swing of it. When you are volunteering as an EMT in a small town, you don't go on that many runs. But it's important to go on as many runs as possible so your skills stay sharp, plus there are continuing education meetings to go to. Long story short I wanted to get back into my rotation quickly so I didn't forget anything and so I was available to learn new things. Besides that, Stormi would have given me an earful if I retired from being an EMT due to her accident. As fate would have it, the first run I went on once back in the rotation involved CPR and we ended up in the same emergency room where Stormi had been. Life sure can play some cruel jokes on you.

There is always something people wish they could go back and change or wish they had done differently. One thing concerning Stormi's visitation I regret not doing is having someone videotape the room where her visitation was after everyone had left. I know there were a lot of flowers, I know there was a lot of memorabilia, I know there were photo collages, but I barely remember any of it. I saw it all, but I don't remember it. I still have and can look at the name tags and cards that were on the flowers, but that doesn't remind me what they looked like or what the room had looked like. I wish I had a video of that room so I could see what a wonderful tribute had been given to Stormi by means of things people made and gave to her. Had a video been taken, it might have taken me months or even years to watch it, but at least I would have had the choice to make. Now, unfortunately, I will never have that choice.

There are things I am very grateful that were done, such as a video being made of Stormi's funeral service. It was quite a while before I was ready to watch it, and it took a couple of tries to get all the way through it, but I have watched it in its entirety. I have actually watched it a couple of times now. Hearing Sharon sing "Jesus Loves

Me" and the pastor's message again were important to me. Once again it's something you can never go back and do if not done at the time. I am also grateful that clippings of Stormi's hair were taken. The way I see it, parents have clippings of their newborn child's hair in their baby books, so there is nothing wrong with having clippings of their hair when they become "newborn" again. The clippings can be put away for safekeeping until a decision is made what to do with them, or they can stay put away forever. But if a parent doesn't think of it before the casket is closed, they will never have the opportunity to decide what to do with them.

I have always been very close with Jamie and Stormi. Except for the normal fights siblings have while growing up, Jamie and Stormi were always very close with each other. In fact, as time went on they even worked together and shared an apartment for a period of time. As I said before, they weren't just sisters, they were "better then best friends." Just two or three weeks before the accident, the girls had had a phrase tattooed on the inside of their wrists, Jamie on her left wrist, Stormi on her right. The tattoo is that of a Dutch phrase *bellus liefde*, which loosely translated means "beautiful love." They had them placed on opposite wrists so they could walk hand-in-hand together as sisters in beautiful love. I didn't know about the tattoos until the day of the accident. Because of the way the bereavement room was laid out, there was only one of Stormi's hands readily available, the left hand. While I had been holding her right hand in the emergency room in Baldwin, the palm of her hand had been down and I hadn't seen the tattoo. At some point in the bereavement room, the sheet covering Stormi was pulled back just enough to expose her hand and the tattoo. Also in that bereavement room, Jamie and Stormi got to hold hands one last time together as "sisters in beautiful love." Jamie had lost her sister and best friend, and I had lost one of my children. I had to remember to not get so caught up in my own grief that I forgot about Jamie's. Jamie and I needed each other more than ever.

Grief is a strange "animal." It can sneak up and bite you when you least expect it, when you aren't even thinking about the reason for the grief. A few months after Stormi's accident, I was standing at a Subway counter trying to decide what kind of sub I was hungry for. I was so deep in thought wondering what would taste the best on that day that I didn't even notice the young lady standing behind the counter. She politely asked if she could help me, and without looking up, I responded that I couldn't make up my mind. Since there wasn't anyone else in line, I took my time deciding. Finally I made up my mind, and I looked up to announce what my decision was. There stood a young lady, approximately sixteen or seventeen years old, with the same color *red* hair Stormi had. Before I could say a word, the floodgates opened up. I composed myself as quickly as I could and explained to her why I was standing there crying like a baby. Thankfully, she was very sweet and understanding of the situation and expressed her sympathies for my loss. I chatted with her briefly and eventually ordered my sub. I had been "bitten" by grief.

One day around that same time, I pulled into the drive-up lane of a local bank. One of Stormi's high school classmates worked at that bank. The classmate and I would joke with each other whenever I came into or went through the drive-up. We would joke about the "message of the day" that was being passed through her, from me to Stormi, or from Stormi to me. It became a little game between Stormi and me to pass fun messages back and forth that way. Just as had happened at Subway, I was so involved with what I was doing that I hadn't looked up to see who was behind the counter of the drive-up window that day. As soon as I had my banking items ready, I looked up to talk to the teller—Stormi's classmate. Just as had happened before, as soon as I saw who was behind the counter, the floodgates unexpectedly opened wide. Once again, I had been bitten by grief. Fortunately for me, this time I was able to conceal it easier. Learning to "live with death" was going to take some work.

Whoever wrote or said "time heals all wounds" has probably never buried a child. I realize that probably wasn't the intent when it was originally written or spoken, but just the same, I don't believe time heals any "wounds." It is my belief that you have to heal them yourself. It is also my belief that if you're going to rely on time to do the healing, then you will be waiting until the end of time to be healed. I don't mean to say that I believe time doesn't help, but left to heal over time by themselves, the wounds, emotional or physical, are going to go nowhere and will leave nasty scars. I firmly believe you have to be proactive. Even with a physical injury or illness, large or small, you will more than likely have to help it along. Scrapes need cleaning, cuts need stitching, broken bones need setting, and appendixes need removing. I think you can see what I mean, that time may help finish the healing process but *you* have to initiate it.

In my mind, the same is true from the "gaping wound" left from the death of a loved one—from the death of a child—from the death of *my* child . . . from Stormi's death . . . from grief. I would have gladly taken any physical wound over the grief I'd been left with after Stormi's death. Even the wounds I suffered when the bull attacked me eventually healed after the doctors initiated the process. But I didn't know how to "heal the wound" of losing one of my children. I didn't know how to initiate the process. I didn't know if it was possible for me to live long enough so there would be enough time for the healing process to be finished.

I decided if I was going to initiate the healing process for the gaping wound I had been left with, I also needed to face my grief head on. I knew I needed to somehow keep my chin up. The way I saw it, "death" had been very "unfair" to me, so I was going to be unfair to death by facing my grief head on. I also realized that even though I was going to take my grief head on, I still *needed* to grieve. I decided it's okay for a man to cry. Not a shocking decision there, but an important one for me. I had cried before of course, everyone has, but never to the extent I have with losing Ma Sue, losing Stormi, and later almost losing Jamie. And I can't say I had ever cried in public before, but that sure has changed. The crying it seems can come at the drop of a hat too, as happened at Subway and the bank drive up window. I think I could be considered a "professional crier" now.

I also know it's okay to have a down day now and then. Everyday life will cause a person to occasionally have a down day. It's not possible for anyone to be on the top of the world all the time, so why would I expect I would always be able to stay ahead of the grief? The trick of course is knowing how many bad days are too many and then doing something about it.

It is important to find something as quickly as possible that makes you feel close to the person who passed away. You're not trying to replace that person, just feel close to them. As goofy as it may sound, that something for me, at the onset, were those Vikings sweatpants. As I said before, they went everywhere I went the first week. For the first while, I needed the closeness to Stormi they represented for me. Slowly but surely I "weaned" myself off them. As time went on, they just laid on my pillow during the day while the bed was made up, and at night they went to the foot of the bed. Then they moved to a nightstand in the bedroom. Now they lay over a large spare-change jar in the corner of the bedroom. I only hold them occasionally now. They may sit without being touched for a year at a time, or they may get held twice in a month. It might be on a "bad Stormi day." It might be on May 8, Stormi's birthday. It might be on November 26, Stormi's "angelversary." It might be on the day I hear of another family losing a child. It's been a "progression" of grieving that has worked well for me. I don't know that others may need or want something as big or obvious as a pair of Vikings sweats, but something as subtle as a picture in a shirt pocket will do. Anything "tangible" that will quickly bring the closeness to a loved one is so very important on the grieving process.

I eventually decided there was nothing I could do to change the situation—the situation of Stormi having died. That may sound like a strange thing to say. I know in the past I would have considered it a strange thing to say—that is until Stormi died. Anyone with any amount of common sense knows you can change some situations, but not that one. You can throw common sense out the window when you lose one of your children, at least for the first while. Because I couldn't change the situation, it became obvious to me that I had to somehow make something good come out something horrible. The hard part was in trying to figure out what good could possibly come from Stormi dying.

As much as I was determined to face grief head on and to win the "battle," I was just as determined to grieve in a way that was healthy to me and respectful to Stormi. You may have noticed that I most often write, "I lost Stormi to a car accident," or "When Stormi had her accident." I don't very often write, "Stormi was killed in a car accident," or say she "died" or that she's "dead." I prefer to say it in a gentler way. That doesn't mean I'm in denial of what happened. Trust me, I'm *very* well aware of what happened. I just don't like "those" words. *But* the cold hard truth of it is, Stormi is dead. There is nothing I can ever do or say that will change that. Time won't change that. Stormi is dead. There are of course multiple ways I can deal with that truth. I could try the "self-medication" method. I could "drink myself under the table" each night to make sure I "forget," or so I sleep well. I could take a bunch of drugs to try to accomplish the same thing. Either way, the next morning Stormi would still be dead. Plus, I would feel and look like crap. And in my opinion, much worse still I would have tainted the memory of my daughter. Or, I could live recklessly and drive fast cars or cycles in an attempt to see Stormi again sooner. Again, assuming I survived my recklessness, Stormi would still be dead. I could just exist and go through life an "emotionless zombie" trying to pretend nothing ever happened. And again, Stormi would still be dead.

The other option is to try doing something positive . . . . I felt I needed to do something positive, something that would allow me to grieve while helping me keep my chin up. I wanted to make some good come out of something horrible. Stormi was still going to be dead each and every morning when I got up, but at least I would be able to look in the mirror and know she would be proud of me with how I handled her passing. I was trying my best to not only do what Stormi would *want* me to do but what she would *expect* me to do. I was trying my best to not let her down. I was trying my best to carry on with life without her. I was trying my best to live with death.

The pastor had said Stormi was a newborn again, so I figured it was just fine if I took "baby steps" in initiating the healing process. I knew there wasn't just one thing that would get the whole process going, that it would take multiple things. It was going to take action on my part because I would have to come up with ideas of what to try. I would have to be patient and understand that everything

I tried might not work. It was going to take hard work because I couldn't just come up with an idea and then sit back. I would have to implement it and then act on it. And I would have to accept that it was going to take the aid of time because it was more than likely going to be a lifelong process.

One of the first things I did was talk to the students at the high school Stormi graduated from. I first contacted the school in March 2006 to see if they would be interested in my idea of my speaking to the students in April at prom time. There had been a number of rumors going around about the accident, and I wanted to dispel those rumors by setting the record straight. I also wanted to "scare the kids straight" so they didn't make the same stupid mistakes Stormi had. I wanted them to know how quickly an accident can happen. Stormi had been drinking and driving, she had been speeding, she had been driving while tired, she had been using her cell phone while driving, and she wasn't wearing her seatbelt. In other words, she didn't one thing right. I was going to try to make something "right" come out of something horrible. I wanted to do what I could to keep another parent from ever going through the same pain I was going through. I was going to try to help myself grieve by hopefully helping someone else.

Only a couple of weeks after I talked to the students was May 8, Stormi's birthday. I knew the first time of her spending her birthday in heaven wasn't going to be an easy day, and it wasn't. I was at the cemetery six times that day. I was so confused and lost that I didn't know what to do. But then a thought occurred to me. There'd been cake for birthdays before, so why couldn't there still be? There were balloons for birthdays before, so why couldn't there still be? So I started a tradition that I have continued on every May 8 since and will do until I spend my birthdays in heaven: I go to the cemetery with cake and balloons. Anyone and everyone who wants to stop and share a piece of cake and their favorite "Stormi story" is welcome to do so. I always make sure the cake I get has plenty of purple frosting on it. I always leave on a paper plate a piece of cake with plenty of frosting on it for Stormi next to her headstone. I tie the balloons to the stand that holds her flowers. I "celebrate" her birthday with her. I laugh. I cry. I grieve. I heal. Where Stormi is buried happens to be close to a busy highway. Judging by some of the looks I get from people in passing cars while I'm standing there in the cemetery with cake and balloons, my method of grieving might not be for everyone. But then again, maybe those people get to celebrate their child's birthday in person . . . what I do works for me.

There are a few other things I started fairly soon after Stormi's passing and continue to this day. I wear a purple rubber memory bracelet on my right wrist. It was something one of her friends had made. I am on my second bracelet, and it has not been off my wrist for more than two years. On the same wrist I wear a second bracelet made out of stainless steel. It's U-shaped so that it slips onto my wrist from the side rather than from over my hand. The two ends of the U have chambers that are capped with Stormi's birthstones. Inside the chambers are clippings of Stormi's hair. I also had a tattoo done on my right upper arm. The design is an idea Jamie had, and my fiancée bought the tattoo for me for my birthday. The tattoo is of a cross. On the vertical member of the cross is Stormi's name. On the horizontal member of the cross is Ma Sue's name. The S of Stormi and of Ma Sue is the same, where the two members of the cross intersect. Each of these items is a way to help me feel close to Stormi. Feeling Stormi close helps me heal.

Working on this book has been a great help with my grieving process. It's an excellent way for me to vent. It's a way for me to show the love I had and will always have for Ma Sue and Stormi. Later on it would also become a way for me to show how very proud I am of Jamie and how much I love her.

A few years after Stormi's accident came another step in the healing process when I formed "Life Wins." Life Wins is an organization whereby I go to high schools and talk to students about Stormi's accident. On an overhead screen I show the same pictures I showed at Stormi's high school five months after her accident, plus some more. I give *every* last detail of her accident and don't leave anything out. Because Stormi did so many things wrong that night, I believe I have a great "platform" to speak from, and I talk about every one of the things she did wrong. I explain to the students how far your car travels every second at seventy mph. I even measure the room I am speaking in so I can physically show them how far that is. Most times the room isn't even long enough to fully illustrate the distance; that really gets their attention. I bring a student up on stage to demonstrate how fast five seconds, the approximate amount of time Stormi had to react to the situation, goes by. I talk about the fake ID she had and explain why it is such a stupid idea to have one. I describe to the students and show pictures of how I now "celebrate" her birthdays. I don't leave anything out. I believe that a real live dad standing in front of students talking about his own daughter dying can make an impact on them. I set up a Life Wins website so students will hopefully look at it after I have talked to them. On the website, I offer a "Safe Driving Promises" sheet that is intended for students to sign along with their parents. My hope is that it will help facilitate conversations between parent and child about safe driving decisions. I feel that if even one student makes better driving decisions and is safer because of it, then the sting of Stormi's death will be just a little less painful. It's my passion or desire to speak to students full time via Life Wins. Unfortunately, I am not in a financial situation at this point where this is possible. It gives me something to strive for in the future.

People have asked me how I can talk about the accident that claimed the life of one of my children in front of large groups of people, and I counter with, "How can I not do it?" Stormi would have done great things with her life. I believe that through Life Wins she still can and does. And I believe that while Stormi is "helping" students make good driving decisions, I can help myself heal at the same time. I don't know that Stormi would like me talking about her in front of large groups of people, but I know she would be darn proud of me for doing it.

It isn't possible to always be upbeat after losing a child. It wasn't always possible to be upbeat before I lost Stormi. But I felt I owed it to Stormi to do the best I could because it's what she would expect of me. And I owed it to myself because it would be the "healthy" thing to do. I had accepted the fact that Stormi died. I felt I was doing pretty well with facing my grief head on and was doing a good job of keeping my chin up. I also believed that, based on my out-of-body experience, Stormi is doing just fine in heaven.

I wanted to come up with something that pulled it all together. I wanted something that pulled together all my thoughts or feelings on how I *needed* to respond to Stormi's death. I wanted something that spelled it all out. It took a while, but then there it was, clear as a bell. Something that pulled it all together, something that made it all make sense. As it turns out, the whole time I was looking for it, it was right under my nose.

I call it **CHIN UP: C**hildren on **H**eavenly **I**sles **N**eed **U**pbeat **P**arents. For me, it says it all. There nothing on this earth that is more precious to parents than their children. They love them, they nurture them, and they base their lives around them. When that child's life ends all too soon, it's a devastating blow. The desperate feeling of wanting to "trade places" with their child is overwhelming. The grief at times is unbearable.

Eventually, there came the realization for me that Stormi is in a better place, that place being heaven, of course. I knew as soon as I lifted Stormi's eyelids that she was "heaven bound," but knowing that doesn't mean it made me feel any better for the first while. Just as any parent would feel, I wanted her here on Earth with me, not in heaven. As soon as the shock of losing Stormi started to fade and reality set in that she was gone forever, I decided that if she did have to be someplace else, heaven was the best place to be. My out-of-body experience can't even be considered a "sneak preview" of what heaven must be like. Take the best, most perfect day you've ever had in your life, and that's what every day must be like in heaven. No pain, no sorrow, only joy.

When I think of the word "isles," I think of a vacation spot like no other. I don't think of just *any* island, I think of *the* island. The island everyone wants to go to, and no one wants to come back from. I think of an island full of docks where you can sit and dangle your feet in crystal clear water, never too warm and never too cold. I think of an island that has more beauty than eyes can perceive; I think of the perfect place, the ultimate vacation spot. One can only imagine what an isle would be like if it was a "heavenly isle." Any parent would rather have his child with him instead of "living" someplace else, but if it can't be that way, then I would think any house number on "Heavenly Isle Drive" is the perfect place for the child to be living. Knowing Stormi and the mischief she occasionally liked to get into, I'm sure she ended up with a "house" right next door to the "detention center."

As I have said, there is no way possible to be happy or positive all the time, not in everyday life, and especially not after losing a child. Stormi can't physically see if I am sad, but I do believe she can still "see" me from heaven and knows when I am feeling down. Even without the belief that she can still see me, I believe I owe it to her memory to be as positive as possible, as much of the time as possible. I am not doing her memory any justice by being negative or down all the time. I am not doing myself any good being negative or down all the time. Stormi needs me, and I need me to be upbeat.

Part of being a parent is setting good examples. I can't set examples for Stormi any more, but I can set examples on her behalf. I can accomplish that by my Life Wins presentations and doing what I can to ensure other kids don't make the same mistakes Stormi did. I can live the kind of life Stormi would be proud of if she was standing right next to me. I can "show" Stormi that while it's not the way I wanted life to be, I will do my best to "carry on" without her. I will do what she would expect of me and keep my *chin up*.

Dictionaries are full of words. Some words have only one letter in them, others have many. Some words have origins that go back thousands of years. Others such as "computer" are new words for new inventions. There are words that are easy to pronounce, and there are words that are difficult to pronounce. Thousands upon thousands of words spanning thousands of years, and yet not a word in any dictionary that can adequately describe the pain of losing a child.

I miss Stormi tremendously. The quote "'Tis better to have loved and lost than to have never loved at all" by Alfred, Lord Tennyson comes to mind. I would give anything, including my own life, to have Stormi back. I am heartbroken beyond any descriptive word there is or ever will be that she is gone. But for eighteen years I had the most incredible love any person can ever experience, the love of a parent for their child. Because of that love, I have memories that I will take to my grave. Because of that love, I have "pictures" in my head that can't be lost or erased. As much as it hurts to have lost Stormi, I would never give up the love I had just because of the pain I have.

I will close this in the same way I always end the "memorial" paragraph or two I put in the local newspaper each year for her birthday:

"Behave yourself, Stormi, and say hi to Ma Sue for me.

Love,
Dad."

Do you remember what life was like before the birth of your first child? As parents-to-be, you lived "carefree" lives. You came and went as you pleased and did what you wanted, when you wanted. You went to bed when you wanted, you got out of bed when you wanted. Unless you had pets that needed tending to, you had no responsibilities to anyone or anything but yourselves. Life was simple; life was good.

Unless you are blessed with an unexpected surprise, at some point in time you decide it's time for a family. You spend a period of time trying, or letting nature take its course, and when it happens, it happens. Life is still simple and maybe even kind of fun at this point, still with no one to worry about except yourselves.

Then came the exciting news: "We're going to have a baby!" You jumped for joy, you danced in the streets, you sent out press releases. I'm exaggerating (maybe), but you know what I mean. The excitement was unbelievable. You hadn't been this happy since way back to the day you first realized you were in love with the other parent to be. There was a lot of planning to do now, a room to get ready, names to think of, clothes to buy—the list goes on and on. But life was still pretty simple. While there were technically three of you now, there were still only two of you in the house. The mother-to-be had to take care of herself, but the "two" of you could still do what you wanted, when you wanted.

Next was the blessed event itself, the "new" happiest day of your life, the birth of your child. There is nothing more miraculous on this earth than the conception, womb development, and birth of a child. What was months, possibly years "in the making" was now, in just a matter of hours (hopefully hours and not days) a bundle of joy in your arms. Now you really did call everyone and their uncle. You handed out cigars. Family and friends came to the hospital to see the newborn and congratulate you.

You stood at the window of the nursery for hours staring at the little life you had created, and you held the newborn as much as possible. More than likely a few tears of joy and pride ran down your cheeks more than once those first couple of days. You thanked your partner from the bottom of your heart for the most wonderful gift you had ever been given.

Now the big change—no, now the *huge* change. It couldn't be any more obvious if it hit you right in the face. It's there as soon as Mom and baby are released from the hospital. Two of you arrived, three of you leave. It's your first experience of putting your child into a car seat, your first time of driving your "family" home. Everything is different now. There are three of you going in the house. That in itself can take your breath away: the first time walking into your home knowing you're now responsible for the well-being of a new life. The long sleep-deprived nights are just getting started, the bottles, the diapers, the teething. There will probably be times of "what was I thinking? I'm not ready for this!"

But it doesn't stay that way. Your baby starts to smile and laugh out loud. There's the age when she only wants Mom or Dad to hold her. Then she starts to walk and talk. Pretty soon there's a little "mini-me" walking around. You see the personality similarities between child and parents, and sometimes that makes you proud, sometimes it scares you silly. You're so proud of your child. Your thinking has changed, and now its "why did we wait so long?"

Your child grows and starts going to school. You start going places and doing things together, things your child can participate in. Your child is now an extension of yourself. Your daily routine revolves around your child's life just as much as it does around your partner's. You burst at the seams with pride each time your child reaches milestones in her life. You can't imagine life without your child. In fact, you have completely forgotten what life was like before having the child. And the process is repeated each time any other children are born. The "individuals" become a "family." Whenever a member of the family is hurting or ill, the other members hurt. It's "all for one and one for all."

Losing a child is just like that, except exactly the opposite.

Whether the loss of your child was expected, as with an illness, or unexpected, as with an accident, the news is devastating. When your child was born, you were excited to call people and tell them the great news, and now it's a struggle to pick up the phone. You may even have to have family or friends help make some of the necessary calls for you. You wanted and chose to have a family, but you didn't want or choose this to happen. What was once joy that didn't have a top is now sorrow that doesn't have a bottom.

The excitement of coming home from the hospital with a newborn in a car seat has changed. This drive home from the hospital is the longest of your life. It may have been many years since the first trip home from the hospital, but if you look in the rear-view mirror, you can still see that car seat in your "mind's eye." But it's not really there, it's been replaced with a big empty space, a space that's as big as the hole in your heart.

The first time walking into the house with your newborn was pure heaven, but now walking into the house is pure hell. Your breath is taken away again, but for all the wrong reasons. Instead of hearing the sounds of crying coming from a child's crib at night, instead of lying in bed at night waiting for the sounds of a teenager coming home, you hear nothing at all. Nothing, that is, but the sound of your own crying. You spent weeks, even months, getting a room ready for your newborn to come home to. Now it's a room you struggle to even walk past. The feeling of "I'm not ready for this" is back with a vengeance. This time the feeling never changes.

Before, you and your child chose clothes together for her first day of school. Now you have to choose clothes for your child yourself, clothes the child will wear for eternity. Family and friends come to visit again, but this time they bring their condolences. Instead of standing in front of the nursery window at the hospital with a few tears of the joy of new life running down your cheeks, you're standing in front of a coffin with tears that have the sting of death in them. And it's not just a few tears, it's more tears than you thought were humanly possible. You want to pick up your child and hold her the same way you used to, but you can't . . . never again.

The days, weeks, and months that follow the funeral are horrible at best. You struggle to eat and sleep. You can't concentrate. You don't want to go back to work, but you have to. You don't want to be around people, but you don't want to be alone. You wonder if you will ever smile or laugh again. You miss the daily routine of your child coming home from school, or the daily phone calls and weekly visits. You put it off for a while, but eventually you have to decide what to do with your child's clothes and personal items. The activities you did together continue on for others, but not for you. As time goes on, you struggle as your child's friends reach milestones in their lives that your child will never see.

You feel as if a big part of yourself has died with your child. The "extension" of yourself that was your child has been removed. And you're not the only one hurting; all the other members of the family are hurting as much as you are. You try to be strong for the whole family, but it's hard to do when you're struggling yourself. It truly was "all for one and one for all."

The emptiness that is felt in your heart and in the home is overwhelming. The freedom that you once knew of not having anyone to worry about except yourselves is now gut-wrenching loneliness. And then it all comes roaring back to you what life was like, what life was like before the birth of your child. And there is nothing carefree, simple, or good about it.

There is no greater joy in life than the birth of a child.
There is no greater sorrow in life than to have to bury that child.
—Me, 2006

Def Leppard

I turned fifty in February 2010, but you would never know it by the music I listen to. I am stuck in the '80s—'80s rock, that is. Don't like country, hate rap, can't stand most pop '80's rock, that's it. Maybe being fifty and listening to '80s rock does make sense, since most members of '80s rock bands are at least fifty themselves. My girls have always known what my choice of music is. They of course had a different taste in music. We would be driving down the road and they would try to put their "crap" music on the car radio and I would simply tell them, "My car, my music; your car, your music." Every once in a while they would try to sneak one past me and have their station tuned in before I got in the car. That would last about three notes before the station got changed. It got to be kind of a game between us to see if I would notice.

I first saw Def Leppard in concert in 1983. That was the first of nine times, so far. On that tour, they were the opening act for Billy Squire. That was the only tour in which they were an opening act, and they have been headliners ever since. I had only heard one or two of their songs before going to that concert, but I was hooked by the time I left. I have bought every album or CD since. As far as I am concerned, Def Leppard is the world's greatest rock band—sorry, Stones.

The girls grew up knowing how much I enjoyed Def Leppard. I listened to their music, wore their T-shirts, read articles about them, watched their videos. I'm not sure, but I might be a bit of a freak. I say that because there was an occasion in July 2004 when I got kicked out of Rock Fest in Cadott, Wisconsin. A friend of mine works for a sponsor of Rock Fest and had a pair of VIP tickets. Since Def Leppard was going to be there, and he knew I was a fan, he asked if I would like to go—a no-brainer. We ended up sitting in the forth row right in front of center stage. I thought I had died and gone to heaven. Def Leppard was the last band to play that night. After the concert was done, we decided, I think it was mostly me, that we wanted to meet the band. So we sneaked behind the stage area to where all the band buses were parked. We could see a tent set up with a line of people (who had actual passes to be there,) waiting to get into the "meet-and-greet." My heart was racing as we got closer. I couldn't believe I was that close to meeting the guys from Def Leppard. Then, from nowhere, came the tap on the shoulder. The guy was huge—I'm sure he used to play football somewhere. He asked to see our passes, so we gave him the deer-in-the-headlight look, and he escorted us to the gate. Jamie and Stormi were so proud of their dad for getting kicked out of a concert backstage area at the tender age of forty-four. Like I said, I might be a bit of a freak.

The girls played right along with my liking of Def Leppard music. Stormi even had one of their songs, "Pour Some Sugar on Me" as the ring tone on her cell phone for me when I called her. I thought that was really cool. I didn't even know you could have different ring tones for different people. The girls brought cookies to the Thanksgiving dinner at Dad's house the day before Stormi's accident. Using frosting, they had written lines from different Def Leppard songs on the cookies. "Pour Some Sugar on Me" seemed especially fitting on a sugar cookie. It made me feel really good that they cared enough about me to do those things. Whether they really liked Def Leppard music or not didn't matter because they loved me.

The summer of 2005 brought Def Leppard to St. Paul, Minnesota. I asked the girls if they would like to go to the concert with me, and they said sure. I told them the tickets were my treat; they just had to take off from work. The concert was outdoors at a baseball stadium. The tickets were general admission, so the earlier you got there, the better the seats. Actually, in our case, the better the place to stand because we ended up on the playing field itself. There were four friends who went along and we arrived plenty early, bringing food and a grill. If I remember right, we were there about two hours before the concert started. I had worn one of my older, faded, and torn Def Leppard T-shirts. Jamie had made her own shirt and it looked really cute.

In order to get the best "seat" for the concert, someone needed to be in line waiting for the gates to open, and Stormi volunteered.

She set up her folding lounge chair and made herself at home. True to her nature, she befriended anyone and everyone she talked to, and "beheaded" anyone who tried to cut in front of her. Jamie helped with the cooking and traded places with her sister a couple times. I made sure none of the "young bucks" who were there got too close to my babies.

The concert was excellent as always. Def Leppard was the last of three bands to play. I have a number of pictures of the girls and myself that night. I have one I really like of Jamie and me standing arm-in-arm in the parking lot. I have one of Stormi and me sitting on a blanket on the ground between bands. I have my arm around her, and she's leaning into my shoulder. It's the last picture I have of her and me together. It was great watching the girls sing along to songs. They actually knew more lyrics than I thought they would.

Also attending the concert were twin sisters about my age. They stood behind us the entire night. We talked some, and they told me a couple of times how great they thought it was that teenage kids would go to a Def Leppard concert with their forty-five-year-old dad. I couldn't agree more. I had the time of my life. I had gone on weeklong vacations with the girls over the years, but I got as much enjoyment out of the seven or eight hours that day as I ever did in a week's time. The girls actually had a good time; they told me they did. It wasn't their favorite kind of music, but they did it for me. We got to talk together, we got to laugh together, we got to sing (or at least try) together. I have my last pictures of the three of us together because of that concert. I have the *last* picture of Stormi and me because of it. I can't begin to tell you how much those pictures mean to me. I also have a lot of "pictures" in my head that can never be erased or lost.

While there were tens of thousands of people at the concert that evening, as far as I'm concerned there were only three. The guys from Def Leppard have played for millions of people. They have no idea the three of us were there; we were just part of the crowd. Their part of the show lasted maybe two hours, but it produced memories for me that will last a lifetime. I had no idea at the time how important those memories would end up being. Who would have or could have known that that concert, other than Thanksgiving dinner, would be the *last* activity the three of us would do together . . . *ever*?

It just goes to show that whether you're "rock stars" like them, or an "'80's music freak" like me, you never know when you're going to provide someone with lifelong memories. As in this instance, with the guys from Def Leppard, you may never know that you provided someone with those memories. And if invaluable memories do occur, who knows when? Will it be today? Will it be sometime down the road? Or could it have been five months earlier on the playing field of a baseball stadium . . . ?

From the chorus of the Def Leppard song "Two Steps Behind":

"Whatever you do
I'll be two steps behind you.
Wherever you go
and I'll be there to remind you
that it only takes a minute of your precious time
to turn around
and I'll be two steps behind."

In "heaven time," Stormi, I'm only two steps behind . . .

Tony

By this point in my life, I knew all too well that lives can and do change in an instant. It was early evening on a Friday in June 2008, and lives were about to change. My ambulance pager went off for a two-vehicle accident about two miles outside Woodville. The page indicated that there was one unconscious patient. I wasn't on call, but I wasn't busy with anything, so I decided to go. I knew that if I went directly to the scene of the accident, I would be able to get there much faster than if I went to the ambulance station, got changed into car accident gear, and rode with the ambulance. I headed toward the accident.

When I got to the scene of the accident, I could see that it had occurred at an intersection. There was a pickup truck with front-end damage on the road. There were a few people standing in front of the truck, but it didn't appear that there was anyone in the vehicle. I then looked to the car that had ended up in the ditch. I could see it had major damage to the driver's side. As I headed toward the car, I saw someone slumped over in the passenger seat. I assumed this was the unconscious patient referred to in the page. My heart and my feet sped up a notch or two.

As I approached the driver's side of the vehicle, I saw the patient was a male who appeared to be in his late teens. I also could see that he appeared to have been the driver. His feet looked wedged under the steering wheel area of the dash. His body was then slid over so that his butt was closest to the driver's side while on the passenger seat. His upper back and shoulders were leaning against the passenger door at about the height of the bottom of the window. Because of the way his body was positioned, there was only one way for his head to be, tipped forward. His head was tipped forward to the extent that his chin was resting on his chest. Because his body was at an angle to the seat with his head tipped forward, I could clearly see his face. In the couple of seconds I stood there trying to take everything in, I could see one other thing: he *wasn't* breathing. His chest wasn't moving and his lips were starting to turn blue. This young man was in big trouble—you can imagine where my mind was heading . . .

I ran to the passenger side of the car as fast as my legs would take me. Even if the driver's door had been open, it wouldn't have done the patient any good. As long as his head was tipped forward like it was, there was no way he could breathe properly, even if he had been breathing. He needed to be lying flat, and the passenger door needed to be opened.

Whenever an injured person has any chance of a neck injury, like was possible for this young man, certain precautions are supposed to be taken. The head is supposed to be stabilized and a cervical collar applied. There are exceptions. You wouldn't take the time to put a collar on someone who was about to be burnt in a fire or possible explosion. You wouldn't take the time to put a collar on someone whose heart wasn't beating. You wouldn't take the time to put a collar on someone who wasn't breathing. I didn't even have a collar with me. I wasn't going to wait for the ambulance to arrive to get one. It could be minutes before it got there, and this young man didn't have minutes. Unless he started breathing, and really soon, any possible neck injury wasn't going to matter.

I knelt down alongside the car and slowly opened the door, and he fell limply into my arms. I am right handed, so I cradled his head with my left arm. I had my left knee on the ground with my right thigh and knee under his shoulders. I put my left ear next to his face to listen for breathing: nothing. At the same time I was watching his chest to see if it would rise and fall with breathing: nothing. I also used my right hand at the same time to check for a carotid pulse. *He had a pulse.* It was weak and erratic, but it was there. Thank God, this young man still had a chance. Thing was, his heart wasn't going to keep beating without some oxygen, and he needed to start breathing—right now.

Two of the first things you learn when you take EMT classes are scene safety and BSI. Scene safety is just what it says. You have to make sure the "scene" is safe before you try to help someone. You never put yourself in harm's way. You can't help someone if you get hurt and become a patient yourself. The car was safe the way it was sitting—there weren't any power lines down next to the car, the car wasn't on fire, there wasn't a bunch of broken glass, so I felt safe with what I was doing.

BSI is an acronym for Body Substance Isolation. In other words, staying away from other people's body fluids. It's kind of like scene safety of the body. There are so many communicable diseases out there, you have to be extremely careful with what you come into contact with. Blood, saliva, any fluid can cause illness and even death if a patient has a communicable disease. Putting latex gloves on is one of the first things you do when you get in the ambulance. Depending on the situation, you might even put on a filtering mask over your nose and mouth. Direct mouth-to-mouth contact when doing CPR is something you never do. There are masks and other devices available so that you are protected. Most times when you go on an ambulance run, you don't know the patient. That means you don't know where he's been and what disease he may have. That's why it's so very important to protect yourself.

I didn't have anything for equipment with me, not even latex gloves. Surely nothing for giving this young man some "rescue breaths" to try to get his breathing going. He didn't have time to wait for the ambulance. If I waited to do something, he most certainly was going to be joining Stormi in heaven. He had a little blood on the side of his head but nothing by his mouth. There wasn't time to think, only time to act. I didn't know him, but it didn't matter. If there was any chance I could help keep another family from having to bury a child . . . I knew what I needed to do; it was a no-brainer. No thinking, only doing. I tilted his head back slightly, plugged his nose, and gave him two "breaths."

His chest rose when I gave him the breaths. That was a really good sign because that meant his airway was open and the breaths I had given him went to his lungs. If an airway is blocked, oxygen can stay in the airway or even go to the stomach. I watched and listened. After a few seconds, he took a few shallow breaths. *Hallelujah!* They weren't very strong and they were erratic, but they were breaths. I waited just a little more and decided to give him two more breaths. Sometimes a person's brain just needs to be "prompted" a little to get a body function going again. I gave him another two breaths, and after a short period of time his breathing became stronger and more regular. He was breathing! I wanted to jump for joy but couldn't; he was still in my arms.

Up to this point, everything had happened in about one minute's time. I didn't know how far away the ambulance and rescue trucks were, and I didn't hear the sirens yet. I monitored his breathing and pulse to make sure nothing changed. So far, so good. His heart rate had actually improved now that he was breathing. I couldn't let go of him to physically check, but from what I could see, he didn't have any major external bleeding anywhere. That didn't mean much—there could be a million things going on inside that could end his young life. I checked his pupils and found them to be a little different in size from each other and they reacted a bit slow to light change. That was an indicator that his brain was possibly starting to swell. I knew that wouldn't be a good thing. You can imagine the memories that came roaring back at that point.

I hadn't had any time to this point to think, but now that was all I had time for. Now, for the first time, I looked at his face. I had "seen" his face earlier but hadn't really looked at it until now. Now I looked at his face through the eyes of a parent . . . through the eyes of a parent who has buried one of his children. My mind went a million different directions. I had no idea who they were, but I thought about his parents. I thought about how their son was in my arms and they didn't even know it yet. I thought about how their lives were about to change. Question was, Was it going to be a temporary change or a permanent one? What was his life going to be like if he survived? I thought about the dreams his parents surely had for him, just like I'd had for Stormi. I prayed they didn't end up spending time with their child in the same manner I do with Stormi. I wondered if this young man was "floating" around someplace looking down at the two of us in that ditch.

And of course I thought about Stormi. How could I not think about her? Here I was, in a ditch holding someone about the same age as her who was teetering on that fine line between life and death . . . because of a car accident. I thought about Stormi lying in the ditch with no one there to help her and what could have been if someone had found her sooner. I thought about how cold it was when she was out there. I thought about how much I miss her. I hoped that this young man had a piss-and-vinegar personality like Stormi that would help him fight to live. I "asked" Stormi to put in a good word for him and to send a little help his way.

I tried not to let it happen, but my eyes filled with tears. I desperately wanted this young man to open his eyes, just not right then. I didn't want the first thing he would see was me holding him while crying like a baby. That would be enough to scare anyone. He wouldn't have a clue why the stranger cradling him was crying.

I heard sirens in the distance now. As the ambulance got closer, I said some prayers that this young man would survive. I prayed that he would return to a normal life and live to a ripe old age and get to experience all the joys of adult life—the ones Stormi was missing out on. I also prayed that if he didn't survive, he would at least live long enough for his parents to get to say goodbye while he was still living. I can't begin to tell you how much I wish that opportunity had been there with Stormi.

The ambulance and rescue trucks arrived and took charge of the scene. Rescue personnel secured the scene, making sure it was safe. They got the driver's side door open and freed the patient's feet from under the dash. At the same time, EMTs started with patient care. I filled them in on what had happened to that point. They slid a backboard under him and put a cervical collar on. He was now ready to be placed in the ambulance. I helped carry him to the ambulance cot and then stood back. He was loaded in the ambulance and the doors were shut.

I stood at the back door of the ambulance and watched the fury of action inside. His vitals were checked and rechecked. His clothes were removed to check for further injuries. His pupils were checked. I could see the look of concern on the faces of the attending EMTs. No time was being wasted; everyone had a job to do and they were doing it as fast as they could. I stood there not wanting to believe what I was seeing: another young life hanging in the balance. I thought about this young man, I thought about Stormi, and I wondered if they had known each other.

The ambulance started to pull away. They were headed for the Baldwin Hospital. He wouldn't be staying there long though, a helicopter had been called. He would be going to Regions Hospital from there . . . the same place Stormi went.

I didn't sleep much that night. I tried, but I just couldn't do it. My mind wouldn't shut down. I kept thinking about the events of the evening. I kept thinking about that young man. I wondered if he was in surgery. I wondered if he had regained consciousness. I wondered if he was alive. Stormi is always in my thoughts, but she especially was that night. I replayed the events of her accident, of the hospitals, of the bereavement room, the visitation, her funeral. I prayed that this young man and his family's journey would end at the hospital without ever knowing what a bereavement room is. That they wouldn't be going to a funeral home to make arrangements. That their only reason for going to church would be to be thankful, not for a funeral. My mind swirled . . . I hoped . . . I prayed . . . I cried . . .

* * *

I got to shake Tony's hand in December of that year. It was in the Baldwin-Woodville High School auditorium. There were a number of high school Christmas plays being presented there on that particular evening, and Tony was there to watch one of his cousins perform. As people were filing in and taking their seats before the plays started, I saw a young man coming down the aisle in a wheelchair. I didn't recognize him at first, but I recognized his parents—it had to be him. I watched as Tony and his family went past where I was sitting and headed for the front row. When they got there, the wheelchair was parked and some of his family sat down. Tony, however, did not stay sitting. With a little assistance from his dad, he stood up, took a few small steps, and sat down in one of the auditorium seats. You can't even imagine the smile that was plastered on my face. It couldn't have been chiseled off.

I sat through the plays, watching them but not seeing much of them. I couldn't help but think about Tony up ahead of me. I wanted to talk to him but didn't know if I should. Normally you don't talk to a patient after you took care of him on an ambulance run, but I didn't think this situation qualified as "normal." After the plays were done, I walked down to where Tony and his family were. I introduced myself to Tony as someone who was at the scene of his accident. He asked, "Are you the person who did CPR on me?" I replied, "Yes, I am." He said, "Thank you." I can't begin to tell you how great that felt. Not the fact that he thanked me; I wasn't looking for or expecting that. It was the fact that he was able to say it, that he was able to talk at all, that he was able to get up from his wheelchair, that he shook my hand. What an incredible rush. That smile was plastered on my face again. I know Stormi was smiling down from heaven with an equally big smile. I slept really, really well that night.

*   *   *

I had followed the ambulance carrying Tony to the Baldwin Hospital the night of his accident. That's when I first found out who the unconscious patient was, who Tony is. I saw his dad there and recognized him as the brother of a guy I used to work with. Now I had a name to put with the face. Tony was in the same emergency room that Stormi had been in. It's the emergency room that's closest to where the ambulance parks, so it only makes sense that the critically ill or severely injured patients are placed in that room. I understandably had an uneasy feeling about Tony being in that room. I know it sounds like a strange thing to do, but I stood there "looking" around the room for Tony. I looked in the same way I looked for Stormi and in the same way I have looked for others. I don't know of anyone else who "looks" around the room for "people," but then again, I don't know of many people who were once "floating" around like I was. I guess maybe it's one of those you-had-to-be-there situations to understand. I'd hoped that "wherever" Tony was, he was comfortable and wasn't scared.

Tony was quickly and skillfully prepped by the hospital staff for the helicopter ride to Regions. His parents were told that he had, among other injuries, a critical head injury. His brain was starting to swell. I could see the look of despair and helplessness on their faces. I knew just what they were feeling; I understood the tears. He was intubated so that his airway would stay open. Hopefully that's all the tube would be needed for, insurance. There was nothing more that could be done. Tony needed to get to Regions to receive care from a major trauma hospital.

Tony spent approximately four months at Regions. The first three weeks were spent in an ICU ward, the last two months in the rehab center. I closely followed his progress on his Caring Bridge website. Besides the horrific brain injury, Tony suffered broken ribs and a collapsed lung. The "long and short" of his brain injury was that his brain had "twisted" within his skull from the force of the accident. His brain twisted so severely that even his brain stem was injured, and it resulted in multiple brain bleeds. There was a lot of brain swelling associated with his brain injury and it was touch-and-go for the first couple of weeks. In fact, on the third day after the accident, Tony's parents were told to prepare to move on in life without him. They were also told that if he did survive, it was quite possible he would spend the rest of his life in a "vegetative state." As it turns out, Tony does have the piss-and-vinegar personality I had hoped for, and *he* is the one who moved on in life.

Tony was in a coma for a large portion of the first two months after the accident before moving to rehab. Some of the coma was the result of the brain injury and some of it was medically induced. Comas aren't very often like you see them on TV or in the movies. A patient can be somewhat responsive to family and caregivers and technically still be in a coma. After he made it through the first week or so, Tony's doctors told his family and friends to "interact" with him to help stimulate his brain. By doing so, they hoped it would help determine how much brain activity he had. His family and friends spent many, many hours talking to and "showing" him familiar items to try to help the healing process. Slowly but surely Tony started to respond to some of the stimuli. One of the first items his mom showed him that got a response was his cell phone. I know the "bond" a teen has with his cell phone is a strong one, sometimes seeming as though that bond is as strong as the one between parent and child. Tony is no exception, but there's more to it in this case, and there's another side to the story. His mom noticed after a number of times of giving him his phone that, while still in a coma and unable to do anything but lie there, Tony would somehow get his phone open when she gave it to him. Once opened, he would fumble around the phone key pad until he "found" the number two button. He would then repeatedly push that button. Keep in mind that at this point, Tony was being fed by a tube surgically implanted in his stomach, he couldn't walk, couldn't talk, couldn't *anything*. And yet he found the number two button on his phone. His mom later found out that Tony had the number two button on his phone programmed as the speed-dial connection—to her. From "wherever" Tony was at that point in time, he was still tying to call his mom. A person could write volumes on that story from every direction: physical, psychological, emotional, and so on. I am going to keep my thoughts short and simple. If I was his mom, I would consider that to be a checkmark in the "win" column for me in the "battle of bonds" between teen/parent and teen/cell phone.

Once fully out of his coma, Tony spent many, many hours in therapy relearning to walk, talk, eat—basically relearning everything. He also had some left side paralysis to deal with. What took seventeen years to learn doesn't come back overnight, even if it was "forgotten" in the blink of an eye. And it only makes sense that it is *much* easier to learn when your brain is in a healthy condition, instead of while trying to heal from a near-death injury. Just as his family and friends were there with him at the start of his long journey, they were also there to encourage him all the way through his rehabilitation. Ultimately, it was because of his hard work and determination that after approximately two months of rehab, Tony was able to go back home with his parents. One can only imagine the joy that was in their and Tony's hearts that day, and every day since.

*   *   *

In May 2012 I went to the home of Tony and his parents. I stopped by to ask for their permission to share his story in this book, and I stopped because I wanted to see Tony. It was the first time I had seen him since the high school auditorium. He looked great—no, he looked fantastic! I can't even begin to describe the feeling I had when Tony came walking, by himself, into the room where his mother and I were sitting. What a wonderful sight. Again without assistance from anyone, Tony took a seat at the table, and we began to talk. I couldn't help but think about the last time I had seen him. I still had the vision in my head of him coming down the aisle in a wheelchair and getting help from his dad to sit in one of the auditorium seats. As wonderful as that vision was, it paled in comparison to what I had just witnessed. I now had a new reason to have a smile plastered on my face.

We sat and talked about the accident, about his progress and current challenges, and about what his future holds. Tony remembers nothing at all of the events leading up to the accident. I explained to them what I saw and did when I arrived on the scene of the accident. I told them about my out-of-body experience, which would help them understand why I wondered if Tony was "looking down" at him and me in the ditch. They had known I'd lost a daughter named Stormi to a car accident but hadn't known the details before then.

As for his current challenges, Tony uses a cane for walking because his balance is sometimes a little off. Having the cane available helps him with security/confidence and leverage, as well as with balance. When Tony talks, it's a little slower and more deliberate than for most people. While the thoughts of what he wants to say are in his brain and ready to go, it takes more time and effort for the words to get to his mouth. Also, reading can be a little difficult for Tony, so it's sometimes easier to have things read to him so he comprehends it better. Tony's mom explained that in some situations he's had to relearn what to say and when to say it—the "there's a time and a place" lesson.

No one knows just what the future holds for Tony. Will he walk again without the aid of a cane? Will he be able to get a job and live on his own? Will his speech improve? No one knows the answers to those questions, and while he still faces numerous challenges, Tony has made great progress and continues to work diligently. He goes to physical therapy three times a week at a specialty hospital. The local hospital has a gym with an exercise pool and Tony goes there between therapy sessions to work out. When weather permits, he goes to Pine Lake Pastures, which is a local hobby farm that has a horseback riding program for young people with disabilities. Tony does not sit around and wait for healing to come to him, he goes out and searches for it. He has his down days when he feels a little frustrated with what has been "dealt" him. It's more than understandable that he would occasionally feel that way, but Tony does a great job picking himself back up. He feels that he was given a second chance in life and believes he owes it to the people who helped him along the way to do the best he can. Simply amazing. With that kind of attitude and motivation, Tony will surely continue to do better.

I am ecstatic that Tony survived. I am ecstatic that his parents don't know the pain of burying their child, their only child. That doesn't mean they don't face challenges because they do; Tony does. But in this case, challenges are a great thing—they're way better than the alternative.

I am so thankful I was there for Tony the Friday evening of his accident. Anyone with CPR training could have done what I did; my part was just a matter of being in the right place at the right time. My feeling of *not* being in the right place at the right time for Stormi has tormented me since her accident. Even though my brain knows better, my heart still feels like I let her down. It is my belief that Stormi "prodded" me to respond to the pager going off the night of Tony's accident, that she prodded me to go directly to the accident scene instead of to the ambulance garage, that she was "sitting" in the ditch with me giving me the courage to do the right thing at the right time for Tony. While my first meeting with Tony had been horrible, the other two times have been an incredible rush. Now each time I see him, or even think of him for that matter, I get to "see" a little of Stormi's piss-and-vinegar personality, attitude, and determination. I get to feel in my heart that Stormi and I were at the right place at the right time together, and I didn't let her down.

I miss Stormi in a way that only another parent in the same situation can understand. I don't understand the whys and why nots for Stormi any more than I understand them for Tony. I don't know that I, or anyone, is supposed to understand them. If everything truly happens for a reason, we need only to look for that reason. And make the most of it.

Tony walked the very fine line between life and death. There was a battle, and the outcome couldn't have been any better. Tony won. His family and friends won. Life Won.

Life: Jamie Rae

I remember reading news stories and seeing news reports on TV of the things people were going to be doing on Wednesday, September 9, 2009. People were going to get married that day, buy lottery tickets, go to the casino, buy a house, anything they felt required a little extra luck. Why that day? Because they thought there was relevance to the numbers 09/09/09—the numbers for the month, date, and year for that particular day. They felt it was going to be a "lucky" day. That day didn't turn out to be such a lucky day for Jamie. She should have stayed in bed . . . literally.

* * *

There had been a phone call. The kind of phone call you receive where you get too much but not nearly enough information. The kind of phone call that scares the daylights out of you. The phone call no parent ever wants to get. The phone call that brings back a flood of memories you wished didn't exist. The phone call that tells you your child has been badly injured.

* * *

Jamie had been taken right to an emergency room. The rest of us had to go through security and get name tags. It didn't take long, and her mother and I were being led to where Jamie was. But I could have walked there myself; I didn't need a guide. I had been there before, I had even been there in my nightmares. It was the same long maze of hallways leading to the emergency rooms. It was the same cluster of emergency rooms where Stormi had been. Within eyesight was the same bereavement room where the family had gathered to be with Stormi after she was pronounced deceased. I was getting really tired of adding to my list of "longest walk of my life" walks.

As I was walking toward the emergency room where Jamie was, I was trying to be strong like she was. I was trying so hard to be positive for her, but the tears ran . . . *she's going to be okay* . . . flashbacks . . . *she's going to be okay* . . . flashbacks . . . *here we go again* . . .

Jamie Rae

J amie was born January 24, 1985. That was about eleven days later than she was supposed to be born. Jamie tried to arrive even later, as her mother had been in labor for twenty-seven hours before Jamie was ready to make her grand entrance. The anesthesiologist was standing by in the delivery room ready to do what was necessary so Jamie could be removed from her comfort zone. That wasn't needed, though. Jamie ended up being born the old-fashioned way.

I'll never forget holding Jamie for the first time. What an incredible feeling. I couldn't get over how tiny she was. At eight pounds, three ounces, I don't know that her mother thought she was all that tiny after twenty-seven hours of labor, but I did. The thought of holding someone so helpless and completely dependant upon others was overwhelming. That moment would come rushing back to me some twenty-four years later. The next "moment" would be completely turned around, though; I would be the one feeling helpless and dependant upon someone else—and Jamie would be holding my hand.

Her mother never had an ultrasound to determine the sex of the baby. I wouldn't have wanted to know anyway; that would have taken some of the fun out of it. Just the same, we did try some of the do-it-yourself methods of figuring it out, such as the needle on the end of a string waved over the wrist. It doesn't work. Jamie wasn't a boy like the "needle" said we were going to have. Had the needle been right, "his" name would have been Joshua.

Jamie was born with a head full of black hair. It turned blond after the first few months without much of it falling out first. Some of her hair was actually part black and part blond at the same time.

I'm pretty sure people would have to pay a good amount of money for that look nowadays.

I can still remember how scared I was. I was a dad; her mother and I were parents. Life was never going to be the same—everything had changed. I was now responsible for someone's life besides my own. It was up to her mother and me to "mold" this new life into an adult who would be a good and honest person. It was up to us to protect her from the world. All anyone has to do is to listen to stories in the news to realize what a scary thought that is. It used to be so simple to go someplace with two people, and now there were three of us. This new third person was a *lot* of work: car seats, diaper bags, bottles, so many things. It didn't take long to figure out that the big *two*-door Ford T-Bird I had bought because I thought it would make a safe family car wasn't such a good idea. The car seat and luggage that went along with a baby was a real pain to get in and out of the back seat. It wasn't long before there was a *four*-door car sitting in the driveway too.

I had always wanted to raise my children on a dairy farm. I wanted my kids to grow up in the same manner I had. I believed it contributed to a close-knit family when everybody was working together on a farm. I thought growing up on the farm helped teach a good work ethic. Besides that, I enjoyed the work. Problem was, I got scared. I was scared that I wouldn't be able to support my family. The prices being paid at the time for crops and milk were terrible. I didn't just have myself and a wife to worry about anymore; I now had a child. I sold my interest in the cows to Dad when Jamie was a month old, and I haven't milked a cow since. I tried car sales after that because that's what Grandpa Zevenbergen had done after farming. Car sales lasted for years for Grandpa, but they only lasted about ten months for me. I enjoyed working with the customers, but I didn't like the way management handled some of the behind-the-scenes stuff. From there I went into construction, which turned out to be some real clear thinking with the way the economy has been since 2006.

While I was working at the dealership selling cars, it was time for Jamie's first professionally taken pictures. There was a large mall that was a ways from home but close to where I worked.

Inside the mall was a store that was part of a national chain of photography studios. Her mother and I decided to have Jamie's pictures taken there. We were both there while the pictures were being taken, and of course we couldn't have been more proud of our beautiful little girl. They took multiple poses and told us that when the pictures were done, we could pick from the poses and mix-and-match the photos to make up our own package. When the call came in that the pictures where ready for pickup, it fell on my shoulders to do the mixing-and-matching because I was working that day anyway. I know darn well the lady behind the counter knew *exactly* what she was doing when she laid out all of the poses in front an "unsupervised, first-time dad." After standing there for a while with a "what do I do now?" look on my face, I did what any loving dad would have done: I bought 'em all.

I received the "we don't have the money for that!" combined with the "I can't send you anywhere!" speech when I got home. I thought getting two speeches for the price of one was a pretty good deal, but I kept that thought to myself. Anyway, that was only the beginning. Upon opening the pictures, we found that on one of the pictures, right smack-dab in the middle of Jamie's right cheek, was a big ole booger. Jamie's nose must have gotten wiped before the last pose was taken, and no one had noticed that the remnants of the wiping had ended up on her cheek. I didn't even notice it when I was mixing and matching. That resulted in my getting a third speech, which I had to pay for separately. To this day my nickname for Jamie is Booger Rae.

Baptism day was interesting for Jamie. She "baptized" her baptism dress with a dirty diaper just as we were leaving the pastor's office to walk into the sanctuary. It was the kind of dirty diaper that went . . . well, it went everywhere. There was a fairly quick diaper change and cleanup, but she still managed to see to it that the church service started a few minutes late.

Unlike Stormi, Jamie was only a couple of months old when she started to sleep through the night. After hearing some of the horror stories other parents told of their children not sleeping through the night, Jamie made me think they were just that: stories. Her sister would bring reality back.

Jamie partially grew up in the same way a lot of kids grow up nowadays, at daycare. Her mother and I were both working away from home, so there wasn't much choice; off to daycare it was. The good part was that her mother's day started later than mine, so Jamie, and later Stormi too, didn't have a full day at daycare.

There are many things in life that I will never forget, but one of the most memorable things for me are Jamie's first steps. I know that may sound strange after all that has happened the past few years, but that's the way it is. Maybe it's so memorable because she is my firstborn and I had waited for what seemed like forever for her to walk. Maybe it's because she took her first steps on her first birthday. Whatever the reason, if I close my eyes . . .

Jamie had been walking around furniture while holding on, up to the day of her first birthday, but that was the day she decided to let go. I was sitting on the couch and her mother was sitting in a chair on the other end of the room. Jamie was walking around the coffee table by the couch, and without any prompting, she let go and walked over to her mom. My jaw dropped almost like it was broke all over again. That was one of the proudest moments of my life.

As great as that moment was, it would end up paling in comparison to what happened twenty-four years later.

Just as I remember Jamie's first steps, I also remember one of her first words. It started with an s, had four letters, ended with a t, and there was always plenty of it around the farm. I thought it was funny, but her mother . . . not so much. I took a lot of shit for that and was forced to change my vocabulary.

Because Jamie is the firstborn, she is also the one who "broke me in" as far as parenthood goes. I didn't always know the right thing to do when it came to discipline. I didn't always know who I wanted her to be friends with. It worried me the first couple of times she went on sleepovers. Long story short, even though those are minor things in the grand scheme of life, I quickly came to the realization that parenthood isn't always easy. I also quickly came to greater appreciation of my parents. Jamie is the one who first gave Mom the Ma Sue nickname.

Jamie adjusted well when Stormi was born. There was the normal amount of jealousy a firstborn goes through when she is no longer an "only child," but Jamie loved her sister and they became great playmates. I think because we lived out in the country, the girls grew even closer. There wasn't somebody half a block away they could play with, so it was either play with each other or sit by yourself. That was part of my thinking in wanting to raise my family on the farm—the closeness it helped create.

Jamie must have been around three years old or so when she started cooking. I don't remember the circumstances of why she was there, but she was visiting Ma Sue at the farm on this particular day. The two of them had been out in the front yard together and Ma Sue stepped inside the house for a few minutes. When she came back out, Jamie was bursting at the seams with pride and excitedly showed Ma Sue the "bird soup" she had "cooked." Jamie had cooked the bird soup in the birdbath, and the main ingredient was every last one of the cherry tomatoes from the plant in the yard Ma Sue had been meticulously taking care of. Jamie had carefully mashed all the tomatoes up so the birds could eat her soup. Ma Sue did the only thing a grandma could do—she thanked Jamie on behalf of the birds . . . and took pictures and told stories many times over.

Because the girls' mother and I had bought some farmland from Mom and Dad when we got married, we had plenty of room for animals. We had up to six horses at one point, a dog, and a number of cats. All the animals helped teach the girls some responsibility and work ethic, another part of my wanting to raise the girls the way I had been raised. Jamie developed a fondness for cats while she was young, and it's a fondness she has to this day. I remember one cat we had that the girls called Mamma Kitty. It received that name because that's just what it was, a mamma—many, many times over. Apparently Mamma Kitty didn't have a hard time finding "friends" just because we lived in the country. Anyway, I remember one night that Jamie woke up the rest of the house with a loud scream. Upon running into her bedroom, we found the reason for the scream. Jamie had woken up to find Mamma Kitty in bed with her—having babies. In the middle of the night, it was Biology 101. Mamma Kitty lost her ability to have more babies shortly after that.

Like any other child, it was occasionally necessary for Jamie to attend the "school of hard knocks" while growing up. Jamie had a habit of losing her gloves or mittens. She would leave them on the school bus, on the playground, basically anywhere but on her hands or in her pockets where they were supposed to be. I finally had a talk with her and told her the next time she lost a pair of gloves or mittens, she would be going to school wearing a pair of my big yellow "chore gloves" that I wore while working at my construction job. It didn't take long, and Jamie lost another pair of *hers*. So being the loving dad I am, I gave her a pair of *mine* to wear to school the next day. It was the last time we had to buy her gloves or mittens due to her losing them.

Jamie didn't like having to wear snow pants outside during recess because not all the other kids were wearing them. So she had a friend write a note to her teacher saying it was okay for Jamie to not wear them anymore. The note was signed, "Jamie's mom." You can imagine the smirk on the teacher's face upon reading that note. That teacher was a good teacher, but the school of hard knocks is still the best school.

Jamie was in the forth grade when her mother and I got divorced. The girls moved with their mom to a small hobby farm five miles from the house we had built. It was very hard being away from them, but we spent as much time as possible together, which helped. Some of the horses went with them and some stayed with me. I was glad some of them went with the girls because that meant they still had the responsibility for some of their care.

The girls and their mom lived there for a couple of years and then moved to a town approximately fifteen miles away. That meant a different school district and a greater distance from me. To help make up for the difference in distance, the girls spent an extra night a week with me. I just had to bring them to school in the morning. It was a system that worked as well as it could. Jamie played volleyball while in junior high and I made sure I attended all her home games.

Jamie was a freshman in high school when she came to live with me. Even though I had always been close to the girls and spent plenty of time with them, it was still completely different being under the same roof again—a *great* kind of different. Besides the extra time I was able to spend with Jamie, I was now in charge of more things and was able to keep a closer eye on her. I don't know that that made her all that happy. I think dads tend to sometimes be a little overprotective of their daughters, myself included. Dating was a scary thing, of course—not for Jamie but for me. I made sure I talked to any "young bucks" who stopped at the house or took Jamie on a date.

There was new terminology in the household because of Jamie. "Stink-good" was the name given to perfume. I had to remind her from time to time to "take it easy with that stuff; a little stink goes a long way." It was because of Jamie that I would frequently ask the girls, "When are you going to start leaving your hair the color God made it?" To this day I still ask Jamie that question. Thanks to Jamie, "hair staining" (coloring) and "skunk striping" (highlighting) were household terms. More than once I offered my "duct tape services" when I saw that she had the hot wax heating up for her eyebrows.

While both girls were blessed with "soft hearts," Stormi did her best to cover hers up, but Jamie wears hers on her shirt sleeve. Jamie has always been willing to help someone. Jamie has always been a happy-go-lucky person and has a smile on her face more than anyone I know. She is probably the politest person I have ever met. Jamie remembered her "please" and "thank you" lessons very well. It wouldn't be until years later that I knew the full extent of her politeness, and I was absolutely blown away by it.

Jamie is more of a "laid back person" than Stormi was. Jamie isn't as opinionated as her sister was. Jamie isn't the "bullheaded" person her sister was. Jamie is "slower to anger" than her sister was. It boils down to it being much easier to get Jamie to see things from "a dad's point of view" than it was with Stormi. That doesn't mean it was easy every time. I remember one time when I was having a discussion with Jamie. After numerous unheeded warnings for her to "zip it," I reached out to give Jamie a "melon love tap," the same kind my dad had taught me to appreciate. Jamie moved to get out of the way and hit her head on a closet shelf just as my hand was making contact. It was the end of the discussion, and as far as I can remember, it was the only discussion we'd ever had like that. We still reminisce about it occasionally and at least one of us laughs about it.

Jamie has always been a very hard worker. She got her first job at age fifteen when she started working as a server at the local A&W restaurant. She did a great job saving her money and was able to pay for her first car herself. But before she got her driver's license, Jamie had to learn another lesson from the school-of-hard-knocks. While she was a hard worker at her job, she tended to put some of her schoolwork on a "back burner." When her report card arrived, it would show that she'd turned in some late assignments. As her parent, I didn't like to see that, so I put my foot down. Her next report card was due out about the same time as she would be trying for her driver's license. I told her if her next report card showed up with *any* missing or late assignments on it, she would have to wait until the next report card before I would let her try for her license. Jamie must not have thought I was serious because the report card arrived and didn't look the way I wanted it to. Naturally she didn't like it, but I kept to my word and made her wait for the next report card. That meant another nine weeks of extra driving for me because I had to get her to and from work for that time period. I also told her it was the same situation for the next report card. No big surprise that the next report card was "clean as a whistle," and every assignment had been turned in on time.

There is always heartbreak in the lives of teenage girls, and Jamie's was no different. Jamie decided to be a queen candidate for the annual Syttende Mai celebration in Woodville, the town where we lived. The candidates had lots of hard work to do; they had to find a sponsor for themselves, they had to raise funds, they had to attend a lot of meetings, they had to find a dress to wear to the competition, and they had to write and perform a "commercial" for their sponsor. My construction business was Jamie's sponsor. Jamie worked hard and did a wonderful job with everything, but she didn't make it on the "court." Needless to say, Jamie was heartbroken, and so was I. There is something about seeing one your little girls standing there crying because of a broken heart; that tears a dad's heart apart. She rebounded from it just fine and in her senior year was named homecoming queen.

Jamie had always been artistic and an excellent drawer. Some of the drawings she completed over the years are still hanging in the schools she was attending at the time. After high school, she took a twelve-month course in graphic design and worked as a server pretty much full time besides attending classes.

The girls had planned on going job hunting together the morning of Stormi's accident due to the impending closing of Ciatti's where they both worked. With Stormi now living in heaven and Ciatti's closed, Jamie was left to strike out on her own. As I said before, Jamie has always been a hard worker. The economy was such at the time that there weren't many graphic design jobs available, especially for someone right out of school with no on-the-job experience. So Jamie found a couple of different serving jobs and worked more than full-time hours for the most part.

Just as I had to continue on with everyday life and grieve at the same time for the loss of her sister, so did Jamie. I admired the strength and determination Jamie displayed during and after the loss of Stormi. She has a completely different kind of personality than her sister did, but Jamie is strong too, just not in an open, public way like Stormi had been. I admired her determination to continue on with a positive attitude in honor of her sister and best friend. Jamie was grieving every bit as much as I was. For the most part Jamie still had that wonderful smile on her face each day. There were a few times it was "painted on," but it was there. We talked every day for many, many months after the accident, and to this day, we still at least text every day. There were many tears during some of those phone conversations, but Jamie always assured me she was okay. We occasionally got together at my construction office to talk, and again, there were sometimes tears. As many times as not, it was Jamie telling me everything was going to be okay. It understandably took a while, but soon enough Jamie got that happy-go-lucky personality back. I really admired her strength and determination. Little did I or anyone else know how important that strength and determination was going to be down the road.

Jamie continued to work serving jobs and a couple of temporary placement jobs as well. Over a period of time, she became more interested in staying fit and exercising. I have to be honest here; in no way, shape, or form did she get that interest from me. My longstanding feeling had been that I got plenty of exercise at my construction job. I was tired and sometimes sore at the end of the day, and the last thing I wanted to do was exercise. I'm pretty sure I may have even vocalized my feelings on exercise once or twice over the years. At any rate, Jamie was more sensible about it than I and wanted to exercise and be fit. She joined a local Snap Fitness gym and started to work out. Because she was there on a regular basis, she got to know the owner, Eric. Jamie and Eric developed a friendship that blossomed into romance. Eventually, Jamie moved into Eric's home with him and his then-seven-year-old son, Ethan. Eric needed a manager at the gym where she worked out, as well as a second gym, so Jamie took on those responsibilities. She continued to do some serving as well.

While working at the gyms, Jamie continued her quest for being in "perfect shape." Even though she had never been in track or cross-country in high school, she started to do a lot of running besides exercising. Being that Eric also ran, they had something they could do together as a hobby. Jamie started competing in the running competitions held in four of the area communities when they held their annual festivities. Over a two-year span, Jamie did very well in her age bracket, placing second once, and first every other time. She had been entering the 5K competitions. I wasn't sure just how far 5K was, but I knew it was farther than I had ever run before, at least on purpose. I was proud of her to say the least.

Jamie continued working for and with Eric. She started doing some of her arts and crafts projects again. Life was good, as good as it could be considering what had happened a little more than three and a half years earlier. We had all done our grieving the best way we knew how. There were still occasional "bad Stormi days," and it was still one-foot-in-front-of-the-other some days, but Jamie had shown us that it was now possible to move those feet faster again and still maintain balance. I was so proud of her strength and determination.

It was September 8, 2009. Jamie was working part time as a server at the same place where I had started working part time when the construction industry slowed down with the economy. On that particular evening, she had finished her shift before I did. As was normal, she came to find me. We said our goodnights, we said our "love yous," and I gave her her favorite daddy kiss, a kiss on each check. As Jamie was walking away, I told her I would see her the next day. Little did I know the truth in that statement. Little did I know that my pride in her strength and determination had only just begun.

It was shortly after 10:00 a.m. on Wednesday, September 9, 2009. I thought the number showing up on the screen of my cell phone looked familiar, but I couldn't quite place it. It was the third or fourth ring before I figured it out. I was pretty sure the number belonged to Jamie's mom, Bonny, but I couldn't for the life of me figure out why she would be calling. I answered and I was right, it was Bonny. She asked me if I had talked to Jamie at all that day, and I answered, "No, not yet." Jamie and I talked most every day but hadn't yet that day.

When I questioned why she was asking, she did her best to explain using the information Jamie had given her. Bonny said she had called Jamie just to say hi and that Jamie was acting a little "strange." When Bonny pressed her as to what was wrong, Jamie finally said that she had fallen and hurt her back. After some more prodding, Jamie told her that she had actually fallen during the night, had spent the night on the couch, and that she had also been vomiting blood during the night. Jamie also informed her that she was now on the floor and wasn't able to get up.

Bonny asked me to call Jamie and find out what was going on. She also said she was headed for the house Jamie shared with Eric and his son, Ethan, and asked me to call her back after I had talked to Jamie. I said sure.

I called Jamie and didn't like at all what I heard. Jamie had just started sleepwalking the last couple of years; it wasn't something she had done as a child. Recently she had been getting up during the night for a glass of water, or sometimes it was even for a bite to eat. She would then go back to bed and know nothing of it until Eric told her, or she found an empty glass or plate the next morning. I remember hearing news reports of children who had gone outside in the winter while sleepwalking and suffered severe frostbite. I remember hearing news reports of people who had even driven their car while sleepwalking. I remember hearing of a local man who had died after falling down basement stairs while sleepwalking. But I never imagined . . .

Jamie said she didn't remember what had happened and was recounting the horrifying story as Eric had explained it to her. On this particular very early morning, Eric said it was around 1:00 a.m., she had, apparently while sleepwalking, opened the patio door in the dining room and stepped out. My heart instantly sank when I heard that because the house has a walk-out basement. The dining room is on the main level, and there wasn't a deck or stairs outside that patio door, and the *concrete* patio outside the basement patio door descends ten or eleven feet from the floor of the dining room. None of that adds up to being a good situation.

Jamie said that she had spent the night on the couch, had vomited some blood, and was now on the living room floor. She told me that her back and legs hurt *bad*. She said that not long before her mom had called she had rolled off the couch because she needed to get to the bathroom. I asked her if she could get up or stand up, and she said she couldn't even crawl anymore, her legs didn't work. She said she didn't have any other pain anyplace else.

I looked at my watch. It was now about 10:15 a.m. Jamie said Eric told her the fall had happened around 1:00 a.m. There I was adding up hours in my head again, and I'm thinking, *What is it with my girls?*

I'd heard enough. I told her I was calling an ambulance. She gave me one "but Dad," but I didn't listen. I told her I was on my way, her mom was on her way, and that I loved her. I called Bonny and filled her in on the information that Jamie had given me and that I was calling an ambulance.

I then called Robyn, my girlfriend at the time who later became my fiancée. She was also a fellow EMT and had been an EMT for a little better than fifteen years. I explained to her what was going on and asked if she was able to go along with me, and she said yes. I picked her up at her place of employment and we headed for Jamie's. I hadn't yet called an ambulance because I wanted to be able to get a look at Jamie myself before she was taken to the hospital. Unlike when the bull attacked me, nowadays you dial 911 and they dispatch the nearest ambulance. I knew the ambulance coming for Jamie wouldn't be from Baldwin, it would be coming from Hudson, which is closer. Because I was coming from Baldwin, I wanted to get a head start before dialing 911. The EMT part of me knew the responding ambulance personnel would take wonderful care of her. The dad part of me wanted to get there and take care of her first, before anyone else. I know it was a completely different situation than with Stormi's accident, but there was *no* way Jamie was leaving that house before I held her hand. Really bad memories were starting to creep back into my head . . .

I called Jamie one more time about halfway to her house. She sounded about the same, in pain. Her mother was there now, so that was a relief. I now called 911 for the ambulance. From the point where we were, I figured Robyn and I would get there first, assess Jamie, be able to tell the EMTs a little better what was going on—and I could hold her hand.

We arrived at the house and went in the front door. Jamie was lying on the carpeted floor of the living room just inside the edge of the tiled floor of the foyer. She looked tired and like she was in a lot of pain. She was wearing her night shorts and a T-shirt. I could see some swelling in the thigh and knee area of her right leg. She said her legs and feet felt funny, and they tingled, a painful tingle. I asked her to move her legs and wiggle her toes. She moved them some, but not like normal, especially the right foot. Not a normal amount, not a normal speed, not a normal anything. When someone has a suspected back injury, you ask the person to wiggle his or her toes, and then you touch the bottom of the person's feet to see if he or she can feel your touch. Jamie felt my touch and then some. She let out a bloodcurdling scream because her feet were hypersensitive. She told me in no uncertain terms that if I did that again, it would be the end of me. Just as someone can have no feeling in his or her feet from a back injury, the person can also have hypersensitivity. Robyn and I looked at each other. I mouthed, "Her back is broken," and Robyn nodded in agreement.

Then I remembered Jamie had also said she'd vomited blood. I gently but firmly pushed on her stomach to check for internal injuries. If a person has internal injuries, his or her abdomen will sometimes start to fill up with blood and become painful, distended, and rigid. Her abdomen felt rigid, but because she exercised and ran a lot, she had good, hard abs. There didn't appear to be any swelling in her abdomen. She said there was only a small amount of pain when I pushed. I thought that pain could be coming from her back. I wasn't sure what to make of all that. She said it had been a few hours since she vomited. She said again she didn't have pain anyplace else.

I now held her hand and asked what had happened. Jamie again explained that she didn't remember, but apparently she had opened the patio door while sleepwalking and stepped out. She said the bedroom window, which is directly above the dining room, was open and Eric had been woken by the sound of her body hitting the concrete. He realized Jamie wasn't there with him and jumped out of bed, running to find out what the noise had been and where Jamie was. He found her on the concrete of the patio, and understandably because of the pain, she didn't want to be touched at first. After a short period of time, he scooped her up and carried her in the basement and set her down. Like a hurt, scared, little puppy, she crawled and hid under the pool table. After much coaxing, Eric got her to crawl out and he again scooped her up. He then carried her up the stairs and laid her on the couch.

Jamie said Eric had told her that they needed to call an ambulance, or at least bring her to the hospital. Jamie insisted she was just fine, that she had only "pulled a muscle." I don't know if she really believed that, but she convinced Eric. Jamie's way of being "convincing" may be a little quieter than what Stormi's was, but she still has a way. Eric lost the battle, and she spent the night on the couch. That's when I realized Eric wasn't home. I had been concentrating so much on Jamie that I hadn't even looked around for Eric. She had even convinced him to go to work that morning. She of course didn't tell him everything she was feeling—or not feeling. What is it about women that can get us guys to act like little puppy dogs and do what we're told? It maybe wasn't the time or the place, but just the same I gave her a little piece of my mind for being so stubborn and not letting Eric call an ambulance.

About that time, the ambulance arrived. Robyn and I filled the EMTs in as to what was going on. Robyn stayed with Jamie and helped to get her ready for loading into the ambulance. I stepped into the kitchen and called Eric. I told him he needed to head for the Baldwin Hospital. He was instantly concerned because Jamie had him convinced that she was just fine. I told him there was no way she had just "pulled a muscle." I told him she had some serious problems with her back. I don't think I told him of my belief that it was broken; he had more than enough on his mind. One of the EMTs came into the kitchen to see where Jamie had fallen. She looked out the patio door and down toward the concrete, and I thought her eyes were going to "bug out."

I went back to the living room. They were finishing getting Jamie prepped for the ambulance ride. She had been placed on a backboard for stability, and she had a neck brace on for the same reason. Neither one of these items is at all comfortable, but she didn't complain. Jamie was in a lot of pain, but I was amazed at how strong she was, mentally and emotionally. If she was scared, she sure didn't show it. As much pain as she was in, she was still joking with the EMTs. But it was only the beginning. Throughout the next several months, she was the teacher and I was the student. I learned a lot about strength from her—more than I wanted to know.

Jamie was now in the ambulance and ready to go. A decision had been made to take her straight to Regions Hospital since any other hospital would have just transferred her there anyway. I called Eric to let him know the change in plans. Bonny was understandably upset and didn't feel up to driving her vehicle there. Robyn drove Bonny's vehicle with Bonny as passenger, I drove my truck, and we both followed the ambulance to Regions.

It was a completely different kind of trip to Regions this time. Stormi had been in a helicopter and they were performing CPR. Jamie was critically injured, but she was stable. There were no lights, no sirens, no speeding. The trip was intentionally easygoing so Jamie didn't get bounced around. Still, I couldn't help but have flashbacks to four years before. The tears ran and a huge knot was building in my stomach. There were so many things running through my head. Was her back really broke? Was she going to walk again? What kind of internal injuries did she have? Am I going to lose *both* my children? I said about a thousand prayers. I "asked" Stormi to keep an eye on her big sister . . .

It's all a blur and yet clear as a bell . . . pulling into the parking lot . . . the walk from the parking lot into "that" building . . . the check-in with security again . . . the "seconds are forever" wait . . . the *newest* "longest walk of my life" . . . the hallways, the emergency rooms . . . the doctors, the nurses . . . *Please, God, not Jamie too . . .*

Once again, there I stood alongside one of my children in an emergency room. I was starting to think that maybe *I* had done something wrong to cause these horrible things to happen to my girls. At least they weren't doing CPR this time. At least Jamie was able to hold my hand too, instead of me doing all of the holding. But that didn't mean Jamie wasn't critically injured, because she was.

The "fury of action" inside Jamie's emergency room was a different kind of fury than had been in Stormi's at the Baldwin Hospital. It was a different kind of intense. There were a lot of doctors and nurses again, there were EMTs again, but Jamie was alive. The "fury" was a slower pace.

Doctor after doctor came in and assessed Jamie. Time and time again she had to tell the "new" doctor where it hurt. Because she said her abdomen didn't hurt, she didn't always remember to tell the next doctor that she had been vomiting blood. I made sure they knew about that. That resulted in her abdomen getting poked and prodded. One of the doctors commented on what good physical shape Jamie was in and said something about her abs. That of course brought a smile to her face. The smile didn't last long though because the doctor then asked Jamie if her feet hurt or if she felt anything on the bottom of them. She must have sensed what was coming next because she said, "Yes, they hurt *bad*, and *please* don't touch them."

I too knew what was going to happen next. The dad part of me wanted to grab his hand and keep him from touching Jamie's feet. The EMT part of me knew he had to. The battle within me of dad versus EMT seemed to be off and running again. The doctor was just doing his job; he was just checking to see what sensations she did or didn't have. He touched her feet and she let out that bloodcurdling scream again. My heart let out the same scream, and my eyes filled with tears.

The touching of her feet was the only time I heard Jamie come even close to complaining. For the first while, she was left on the back board. She had the neck brace on for a long time. Either one of those items will cause a lot of people to complain. I know, I've witnessed it. But Jamie handled it very well. While she didn't thank the doctor who touched her feet, it was "please" and "thank you" to each and every other person who was ever in that room. Her ability to have a smile on her face even when the chips were down had always impressed me. Over the next several months I found out that I hadn't seen anything yet.

I stood next to Jamie as much as I could and held her hand. I don't know that the hand holding was as much for her as it was for me. She caught me with tears in my eyes once and reassured me she was going to be fine. So many things were going through my mind, and yet I didn't know what to think. Even though I couldn't think straight, I still managed to fire off another round of a thousand prayers.

Eric had now arrived at the hospital. After talking to him by phone while I was still at his house, he had pretty much dropped what he was doing at work and headed for Regions. I explained to him that shortly they were going to be taking Jamie to radiology for a CT scan. The plan was to scan Jamie from top to bottom to find anything and everything that was broken. The same scan would also show if there were internal injuries that had caused her to vomit blood. I wasn't even done talking and Eric was on his feet heading for the maze of hallways.

Because only two visitors were allowed in the emergency room at a time, Bonny stepped out so Eric and I could go in. Once we got inside, I thought Jamie would get emotional upon seeing Eric. Eric got teary-eyed, but Jamie did just the opposite. I don't know if Jamie realized the gravity of the situation at that point or not, but if she did, she sure didn't show it. Eric went to stand alongside Jamie and held her hand for just a second before leaning over to give her a kiss. Because Jamie was lying flat on her back, she was looking up at Eric's face. The first thing she said to him was, "Ya got a bat in the cave, honey." Eric must have thought Jamie was delirious with pain because he looked at her with a very puzzled expression and said, "What?" Jamie repeated, "Ya got a bat in the cave." She must have realized he didn't have a clue what she was talking about. Finally she cleared it all up when she said, "You have a booger in your nose." It was the first of many times Jamie would use laughter over the next several months to help herself and those around her to heal.

A little more time passed and it was time for Jamie to have her CT scan done, so Eric and I went back out to the waiting room.

Dad and Eric's mom, Sally, were there now. We filled them in as best as we could with the information we had been given, or as we understood it. The two of them were naturally concerned, as were the rest of us. We sat and visited and made a few phone calls to let people know what was going on. Understandably, the subject came up that "we were just here" at that hospital. As I sat there, I couldn't believe what was happening. I thought back to the time of Stormi's passing when a few people had commented, "Your family has been through so much lately. How much more can you handle?" I wondered if I was about to learn the answer to that question.

I don't remember if someone came and told us, or if we walked back to the emergency room and found out for ourselves, but Jamie was now back in the room. We were told it would take a little while to get the results, but she was still stable and we could continue visiting with her, two people at a time. Dad, Robyn, Sally, Eric, Bonny, and I all took turns sitting with her. When Jamie saw Sally, she right away asked, "What are you doing here? You're supposed to be golfing." Even with the amount of pain Jamie was in, even with the uncertainty of what lay ahead, Jamie was still concerned that Sally was at the hospital because of her instead of on the golf course with her ladies' Wednesday afternoon golf league.

I was amazed that, after all that had happened so far, Jamie even remembered it was Wednesday, let alone the fact that she knew it was afternoon. I had lost track of time myself and wasn't even sure whether it was afternoon. Little did we know that the fact that she knew the day and approximate time, the fact that she comprehended everything that was going on around her, the fact that she knew anything at all, the fact that she was still conscious, the fact that she was even alive was about to become an unforeseen miracle.

Dr. Mendez came into the room with the results of the test. Because the room had been a "revolving door" of doctors before the CT scan, I still can't remember if that was the first time we met him or if he was one of the doctors who had been in the room before. Either way, it's my first memory of him. It's also the memory of him that I will *never* forget. The memory comes from nothing to do with what he looked like, it had nothing to do with how he acted—it was what he said: it was the "bombshell" he dropped.

He said Jamie's back was indeed broken. My heart sank, but it was what I already knew. I had known her back was broken since I'd walked into the house and saw her swollen legs that didn't work right. He said it was actually broken in two places, that one vertebra was cracked and the other was shattered. The vertebra that was shattered had fragments that were putting pressure on her spinal cord. He said her spinal cord wasn't cut but was being severely "compromised" by the fragments pushing on it. He said Jamie would be having surgery just as soon as everything was ready to get the pressure off her spinal cord. Even though I knew in my heart that her back was broke, it was still something that "echoed" over and over in my head. I couldn't believe that *both* my girls had suffered broken backs by time they were twenty-five. I was so busy listening to the "replay" in my head of what Dr. Mendez had just said that I had forgotten all about the blood Jamie had vomited. I had forgotten that she must have some kind of internal injuries, even if minor, to cause her to vomit blood. I was so busy listening to the replay that I didn't even see the bombshell coming. Jamie didn't have any internal injuries that caused her to be sick. Jamie had a skull fracture with multiple brain bleeds—three to be exact.

His words ringing in my ears stopped me dead in my tracks. The room started to spin . . . again . . .

I couldn't believe what I'd just heard. I couldn't believe what a horrible dad I was. Worse yet, I couldn't believe what a horrible EMT I was. How could I have missed that? Any "rookie" EMT knows that someone can vomit from a blow to their head. I knew I had asked Jamie a bunch of times if she had pain anyplace else, but I just couldn't remember if I had asked her specifically about her head. I couldn't understand how she could have an injury as severe as a skull fracture along with bleeding on her brain and be as alert as she was. I knew every patient and situation is different, but then I started wondering about the possibility of her brain starting to swell. Depending on the situation, some people's brains start to swell right away, some start to swell later. I thought about Tony . . .

I didn't know what to think or do. One of the nurses must have noticed I was struggling some because she tapped me on the shoulder and offered me a chair. Dr. Mendez started to explain what would be happening in the coming hours, days, and weeks. He said it would be a little bit yet, but they would be taking Jamie to surgery to repair her back. The surgery to repair her back would be done from the front. Because of the location of the fragments that were pushing on her spinal cord, it was necessary to operate on her back from the front. They were going to remove a rib, push her internal organs off to the side so they could access her spine, remove the bone fragments that were pushing on her spinal cord, use the rib that had been removed to "make" a new vertebrae, and install some screws and plates to hold it all together. Dr. Mendez made the surgery sound simple, but I knew it was anything but simple. He said Jamie would be in intensive care for a few days, be hospitalized for seven to ten days, and undergo approximately three weeks of rehabilitation.

He then started talking about Jamie's skull fracture and brain bleeds. He said the bleeds appeared to have happened at the time of the fall, without much change since then. He said there was one bleed in the front of her skull and two in the back and that there didn't appear to be much swelling of her brain. Dr. Mendez said the largest concern for Jamie's skull fracture and brain bleeds at that time was the amount of fluids she would be getting during surgery to repair her back. The concern was that the extra fluids she would be getting could cause the brain bleeds to spread, or worsen. He said her head injury was a very serious injury, but the greatest concern was her back. What? I couldn't decide how hearing that statement made me feel. Jamie had a skull fracture with brain bleeds, and yet there was something worse? How could that be? Somehow, the doctor saying that made me feel a little more comfortable about the severity of her head injury. Because he said that, I hated myself just a little less for not thinking about the possibility of a head injury as well as internal injuries when I was assessing her. But—

Jamie then asked what I had been wondering but hadn't allowed myself to think about: "Will I walk again?" I'm pretty sure at that time the only sound that could have been heard in that emergency room besides a pin dropping was my heartbeat. My heart was beating so hard I could feel it in my temples.

It seemed like forever before Dr. Mendez responded. He told her that anyone he had ever operated on with a broken back who was able to move their legs prior to surgery had some capacity of walking after a period of time. Jamie had been moving her legs some, but I wanted a definition of "capacity of walking" and "period of time." He must have read Jamie's mind, because when she looked up at him after hearing his response, he said, "Yes, I will be operating on you."

Jamie seemed okay with his answer and even thanked him. Even though I had only known Dr. Mendez for a few minutes, I really liked the guy. I liked that he spoke with confidence without being cocky. I liked that he had a game plan. I liked his honesty. I liked that he acknowledged everyone in the room when he talked but spoke directly to Jamie. I liked that he held her hand, and asked her if she was okay. I liked that I liked this guy. It was important to me that I liked this guy. My daughter's life, the life of my only living child, Jamie's life, was about to be in his hands—literally.

There was one more bit of information that Dr. Mendez needed to share. I think Jamie's response to that information was the start of her working her way into the doctor's heart. He said the particular vertebra of Jamie's back that was shattered is where the nerve that controls bladder and bowel functions comes out of the spinal cord. He further said that patients who have broken that particular vertebra with the severity of Jamie's break frequently have "control" issues after surgery. Jamie thought for just a second and then looked at Eric and said, "Are you still going to love me if I pee myself?" It was the moment we all needed. It was the laughter we all needed. It was typical Jamie. It was what Dr. Mendez needed to hear so he knew he had a "fighter" working with him. And I'm sure there was a "hint of honesty" in Jamie's question. She really wanted to know. Eric's answer of course, was a resounding *yes*.

I can only imagine all the thoughts that were going through Jamie's mind. I can only imagine all the thoughts that were going through Eric's mind. I could only imagine what was going through their minds because I couldn't even figure out what was going through mine. All I knew was that I needed to get out of that room for a few minutes. I got up from the chair the nurse had so graciously given me, held Jamie's hand, gave her her favorite daddy kiss, told her how much I loved her and how proud I was of her, and walked out of her room.

Outside her room was a "common area" that was also common to several other emergency rooms. In the middle of the common area was a large nurses' station. I started toward an exit sign. I wanted some fresh air. As I was walking, my emotions started to get the better of me and the tears started to run. A ways up ahead of me close to the exit sign, through my teary eyes I saw the face a man who looked vaguely familiar, like the face of someone I should know. It wasn't until I was past the corner of the nurses' station and could see his *shirt collar* that I figured out who he was. It was the same chaplain who had offered a prayer for Stormi in the bereavement room. He was looking right at me and must have seen how upset I was. As I got closer to him, he started to approach me—oh, great . . . . By the time we were close enough to each other that he could reach out his hand to shake mine, we were only ten feet from the bereavement room. *This day just keeps getting better;* I thought. Either this guy didn't remember our previous encounter, or he was a glutton for punishment . . .

The chaplain didn't remember me. I didn't talk to him about it, but depending on how much he works, he may easily have talked to more than a thousand people since the first time we'd met. He couldn't possibly remember everyone, not even the crabby ones like me. Once I had refreshed his memory with Ma Sue and Stormi and then told him what was going on with Jamie, I'm surprised he didn't duck for cover out of fear of a lightning bolt striking him because he was standing next to a person who was having the kind of "luck" I was.

We talked for a short time and then he asked "that" question again: "May I say a prayer for you, your daughter, and your family?"

All kinds of responses ran through my head, some more "appropriate" than others. I decided it would be best if I took up my "issues" directly with God rather than take them out on this poor chaplain. I also felt like a bit of a hypocrite. I had been saying thousands of prayers myself, so what would it hurt if the chaplain said a prayer? And how could I even say prayers myself if I was upset that God had "allowed" yet another incident to happen? I was a mess, and nothing made any sense. I figured I'd better shape up or that lightning bolt was going to be headed for a bull's-eye on the top of my head.

The chaplain was a good man. He wasn't there just collecting a paycheck, he truly cared about the people he talked to. And in some cases like Stormi's, he also truly cared about the people he didn't get to talk to. Once again, the chaplain did a nice job with his prayer. But God *still* had some major explaining to do.

I went outside and got some fresh air. It felt good, but I don't know that I was thinking any clearer when I went back inside. I say that because of the decision I made when I went in. I had to walk right past the door to the bereavement room on my way back to the emergency room where Jamie was. I don't remember making a conscious decision to reach for the door handle to see if it was locked, but all of a sudden, there it was in my hand. Once I found it was unlocked, I did have a decision to make: "Do I or don't I?" I don't remember my thought process of deciding or if I even had a thought process, but I went in.

A whole flood of emotions let loose once that door closed behind me. There were emotions that were almost four years old that came pouring out. There were emotions that were fewer than twenty-four-hours old that came pouring out. Somewhere in that room, I "heard" Jamie scream Stormi's name twice at the top of her lungs. I had to believe Stormi had screamed Jamie's name the night before. I stayed in the room until I felt drained of my emotions. I was pretty sure there was still more to come, but it was nice to have purged myself as much as I had.

When I got back to the emergency room where Jamie was, Dr. Mendez was out in front of her room looking at some of the CT scan pictures of Jamie. I don't know if he was asking "Dad Jeff" or "EMT Jeff," but he asked if I would like to see some of them. I said sure. Once he pointed out the line of the skull fracture and the shadows of the brain bleeds, I could see them. He didn't have to point out anything once he got to the pictures of her shattered vertebra. I had seen and dealt with a lot of things in my careers as an EMT and as a dad, but this combining of the two had to stop. There seemed to be a million pieces instead of one when it came to that particular vertebra. I remember a "warm feeling" coming over me. I remember starting to feel dizzy, and I remember a chair being pushed under me. Having to sit down twice in less than an hour wasn't doing much for my tough-guy status.

Jamie was scheduled to have an MRI, and then it was time for surgery. I was scared beyond scared to have her headed for surgery. I was thankful beyond thankful to have her headed for surgery—at least she was alive to be headed for surgery. I held her hand and walked by her side as her bed was wheeled to radiology for the MRI. I was amazed at how she continued to stay upbeat despite the pain she was in and despite the uncertainty of the future. I felt she was stronger than I was.

The MRI was completed and it was off to the operating room. There was only a limited time available to say "see you later," and there were other family members who needed their time also. I told Jamie I loved her, gave her her favorite daddy kiss, and stepped aside to make room for someone else.

There were many things I thought about that late morning, afternoon, and early evening. Some were things I had thought about before, some weren't. One thing I hadn't thought much about before was the fact that I wasn't the only "man" in Jamie's life anymore.

Seeing Jamie and Eric together made me realize she was all grown up, she wasn't *my* little girl anymore. It was hard and wonderful at the same time. She still needed her dad, but she needed her "man" too. "Letting go" isn't always as easy as it sounds. Maybe if I hadn't just left Stormi in God's hands, maybe if I wasn't leaving Jamie in the doctor's hands, maybe if I didn't feel like she was all I had left . . .

It was around 7:00 p.m. on 09/09/09, the "lucky" day, and Jamie was being wheeled into the pre-op area where only medical staff was allowed. Jamie's and Eric's families all gathered in the surgical waiting room to wait for news. Robyn and I found a public Internet access computer, opened a Caring Bridge site for Jamie, and wrote the first journal entry. We then went back to the waiting room and I sat for a short time. Sitting there just wasn't working for me, so I decided to take a walk. I walked out into the hall, headed for the exit sign, and kept walking.

I took a left turn once outside the door and kept walking. I walked for Jamie. I walked *for* Jamie for the same reason I had walked *for* Stormi, because she couldn't—at least not at that time. I walked around the outside of the hospital much the same as I had almost four years earlier. I felt overwhelmed because there was so much to think about and try to process. One of the things I thought about was that it had been my dream since the girls were newborns to walk them down the aisle on their wedding days. I was already going to miss that with Stormi. Was I now going to miss it with Jamie too? Then I decided that as long as she was alive, I would be happy to be able to push her down the aisle in a wheelchair. And then just as had happened after Stormi died, I realized I was being selfish. I was thinking about myself and what I would be missing. I needed to be thinking about Jamie, not myself. I needed to be positive for her and support her, no matter what.

It was understandably an uneasy several hours spent waiting for Jamie to come out of surgery. Someone on behalf of the surgical staff would occasionally deliver a message telling us that surgery was going well, but it was pretty much torture sitting there waiting. Other than waiting, there wasn't a whole lot to do; you could "read" the same newspaper for the third time, even though you wouldn't comprehend it any more than you did when you read it the first or second time. There was no way I was going to try to sleep; it wasn't even a distant thought. We mostly just sat there, talked, and took walks by making trips to the vending machines.

At long last, a little before 2:00 a.m., Dr. Mendez came into the waiting room. He told us the surgery had gone very well. He explained everything he had done to repair Jamie's broken back. I think I liked him even more after he had operated on her than I did before surgery. It was obvious he was a very caring and patient man because he took the time to answer all questions, besides explaining what he had done. He told us it would be another one and a half hours before we could see her. He explained that Jamie would be having a CT scan before going to the recovery room to make sure the screws and plates he had installed were in their proper place and alignment. The CT scan would also show if the brain bleeds had changed at all during surgery.

Dr. Mendez continued by saying that Jamie would be in surgical ICU for the first few days. He said she would be in extreme pain during that time. The tests that were done while in the operating room had indicated there was a large amount of swelling in her spinal cord. The tests also showed there was limited nerve function in her right leg. He said the nerve function to her leg could possibly return to normal over a period of time.

Then he said something that really scared me. He said that 60 percent of Jamie's spinal cord space had been occupied by the largest of the fragments from the vertebra that was shattered. It's no wonder there was so much swelling in her spinal cord. It's no wonder there was limited nerve function to her right leg. It wasn't said, but in my mind it was a miracle she wasn't paralyzed. He concluded that he was optimistic that Jamie would walk again, but it was going to take time and a lot of hard work. That was wonderful news of course, but I was a little concerned too. I knew the "hard work" part would be no problem for Jamie, but I was a little worried about the "time" part. Because Jamie was always so active with daily life and with exercising, I just hoped she was going to have the patience it was going to take.

Some family members left after Dr. Mendez finished talking. After all, it was 2:00 a.m., and it had been a "hurry up and wait" situation. There wasn't anything anyone could do but wait. There was no way I was going anywhere, and those of us who stayed wandered around or stayed in the surgery waiting room until we knew Jamie was in the surgical ICU. The surgical ICU waiting room was a smaller room. There were naturally other people in ICU, so we weren't the only family looking for a place to sit. It was first come, first served for seating.

Around 9:30 that morning Jamie was scheduled for another CT scan. They wanted to check again on the positioning of the screws and plates in her back, and check on the brain bleeds. We were told they would continue to do CT scans to monitor those two concerns. Even though she hadn't moved much, if any yet, they still needed to keep a close eye on her back. Everything had to be perfectly aligned before she would be allowed to move much. The brain bleeds were also something that needed to be monitored closely, at least until they got smaller or dissolved. If everything still looked good after the scan, they would start allowing her to be more alert and work on removing the intubation tube that was still protruding from her mouth and running into her throat. I think anyone reading this can understand why it bothered me so much to see that tube in place, can understand why I couldn't wait for it to be removed, can understand why I asked more than once when it was coming out. The EMT part of me knew why it was still there, but the dad part of me just wanted it gone *now*.

Jamie was starting to be a little restless from time to time. At one point she gestured that she wanted a pen and paper to write a note. But by the time the pen and paper got to her, she was sleeping again. Judging by the expression on her face, she was in an extreme amount of pain. As hard as it was to see her in so much pain and seeing all the machines hooked up to her, I was grateful for her pain and for the machines. The pain and the machines meant she was still alive. I still had my daughter.

I happened to be in Jamie's ICU room with her when Dr. Mendez stopped in shortly before 9:30. I was surprised to see him so soon after surgery. It made me wonder if he had stayed awake like most of the rest of us who were still there. If he had stayed awake, he certainly looked better than I did. He said he wanted to stop in and check on Jamie before she was taken to radiology for her CT scan. As we were talking, Jamie opened her eyes a little and got just a hint of a grin on her face when she saw us. As long as the doctor had her attention, he asked Jamie to move her legs. It wasn't easy for her to do, and you could easily see the extreme pain on her face when she moved them, but *she moved them*. I couldn't believe my eyes. The right leg clearly moved slower and less, but they both moved! It was a dream come true, it was answered prayers, it was emotional—it was everything.

The next words out of Dr. Mendez's mouth made my jaw do the "broken jaw flop" again. He looked right at Jamie and said, "I'm sorry, but I wasn't able to do a 'boob job' for you after I was done repairing your back." Upon hearing that, Jamie actually got a sad look on her face and looked down toward her chest. I'm not sure if the doctor heard my chin hit the floor, or if he just figured he should explain that while in pre-op, the always smiling and joking Jamie had asked him, "As long as we're headed into the operating room anyway, how 'bout a boob job at the same time?"

One can only imagine the look on his face and the smile in his heart when he heard that. One can only imagine the fear that was within Jamie at the time she said that. She had to be feeling all of the same fears the rest of us were feeling for her, only worse because it was her body, her future. But Jamie handled her fears in true "Jamie fashion." She handled her fears by saying her prayers, she handled her fears by putting a smile on her face, and then she laughed at her fears. Whether the doctor and the others who laughed at her request for a "boob job" knew it or not, they also "laughed" at her fears. Under the circumstances, it would have just as easy for Jamie to have been an emotional wreck. But that wouldn't have been Jamie, and it wouldn't have done her any good. A good attitude, a smile on her face, and laughter in her heart had gotten Jamie through some pretty rough times in the first twenty-four years of her life. I hoped and prayed she would be able to keep that trend going through the difficult times that were ahead of her. Over the coming weeks and months, Jamie showed me I had nothing to worry about.

The 9:30 a.m. CT scan looked good again, so Jamie was allowed to start "waking up," and by shortly after 11:00 a.m. the intubation tube had been removed. What a wonderful thing it was to see her smile and hear her talk with that horrible tube gone. I don't *ever* want to see one of those tubes again. It's amazing how something can trigger bad memories just by the mere sight of it. That "something" for me was seeing that tube in place in Jamie. There aren't words to express how grateful I was that the order for tube removal from Jamie's mouth/throat was given by a doctor instead of by a coroner.

As the day went on, more of the equipment attached to Jamie was removed. Dr. Mendez's prediction was correct: she was in an extreme amount of pain. The pain meds made her sleepy so she spent most of the day sleeping, but she was occasionally awake. Jamie has always been a talkative person, like me, and whenever she was awake she was talking. She didn't know how much the intubation tube bothered me, so when she kept talking and I thought she should have been resting, I threatened to have them put the tube back in. In all honesty, it was partly the subject matter that made me want her to stop talking because Jamie was talking about walking. She was asking if, how, and when she was going to walk again. They were very legitimate questions that she had every right to know the answers to. Problem was, no one knew—not Dr. Mendez, not Eric, not her mom, not me. All we could tell her was that the doctor was very optimistic that she would walk, but it would just take a while and a lot of hard work. That completely helpless feeling was coming over me again in a big way. The feeling that a dad has that he is always supposed to be able to protect his children from harm, fix anything that's broken, answer any questions they have—in other words, basically be "superman"—was coming at me from every direction. I don't know if I had more expectations over the years of the girls or of myself as a dad. Either way, I wasn't feeling like I had lived up to "superman status." I started looking for that same elusive "door" I looked for so often after Stormi's accident.

On Friday, the second day in ICU, Jamie was started on some anti-seizure medication. My heart sank when I heard she would be receiving that because I assumed it meant they were concerned about her brain injury. They were actually giving her anti-seizure medication to help control the hypersensitivity in her feet. Her feet were so sensitive that at times she couldn't even stand to have the sheets on the bed touch them. That medication made her sleepy so she spent a good part of the day sleeping. During a portion of the time she was awake they started doing rehab work with her legs. It was obviously very painful and hard work to move them, but as I said before, Jamie has never been afraid of working hard. She knew it was going to take a lot of hard work and she was willing to do it. As always, she did it with a smile on her face and said "please" and "thank you" to everyone she came in contact with. She even thanked the nurses when they gave her shots. They also had her blowing into a special metered "box" to help keep her left lung from collapsing. A lung collapsing can be a side effect of a rib being removed. Being the "silly" person Jamie is, she laid the box on its side while blowing into it in an effort to get better results. That not only got a smile out of the nurse but also a "re-do." At one point I asked the doctor how large of a piece of rib had been removed, and he held up two fingers about eight inches apart. I imagine that's about how big my eyes got.

Just as Stormi's injuries had helped explain just what happened during her accident, so did Jamie's. Dr. Mendez explained it this way: when Jamie "stepped out" of the patio door and fell to the concrete, she landed on her feet. Obviously she was very fortunate not to have broken her heels, ankles, or legs as well. At the time she hit the concrete she was leaning forward. That means her spine was rolled forward and her vertebrae were at an angle to each other. We've all heard the old joke or saying, "It's not the fall that will hurt you, it's the sudden stop at the bottom." While that may be an obvious truth, in this case it's also a scary one. Because Jamie's body came to such a sudden stop, and because her vertebrae were at an angle to each other, her vertebrae "hit" each other and broke. As I said before, one broke and another shattered. She also lost two disks because of the fall. The sudden stop is also what caused one of her brain bleeds. Her body stopped so fast that her brain "sloshed" forward and hit the front of her skull hard enough to cause a bleed. (I waited a little while, but being the loving dad that I am, I eventually teased Jamie that had her brain taken up all of the space in her skull that particular bleed wouldn't have happened.)

Jamie then tipped backward and hit her head hard enough on the concrete to fracture her skull and cause two more brain bleeds. I'm not sure if it was the sound of Jamie's feet or head hitting the concrete that was loud enough to wake Eric. I don't want to know. One of the "cute stories" to come out of the whole horrible ordeal came from the thoughts of Eric's son, Ethan, who was nine at the time. He decided he was going to give Jamie the nickname Kitty because he said that anyone who can fall that far and still land on her feet must be part cat. Kids have such a wonderful way of simplifying things. There have been *many* times since 2005 that I have wished I could do that.

The first few days were long ones. I got about forty-five minutes of sleep in the first forty hours after Jamie fell, and at one point someone told me I looked like hell. I thanked him for the compliment because that was certainly better than how I felt. It was difficult to do, but eventually I left the hospital and went home for a night. Eric was there as much as I was, Jamie's mom was there as well, but it was still hard to leave. It was a completely different situation, but while driving, I couldn't help but think about my previous drive home from Regions. There were so many unknowns and yet so much to be thankful for. At least this time I knew I would be bringing my daughter home.

Jamie continued to have frequent CT scans to check her back and brain bleeds. It was decided that she would be wearing a "turtle shell" brace for an extended period of time just as soon as they were able to remove her chest tube. The chest tube went in where the incision had been made to repair her back and needed to stay in place until there was nothing draining out of it anymore. Once the tube was gone, the brace would go on. It was described as a two-piece hard plastic shell with a thin layer of foam lining on the inside, and Velcro straps on the outside that would hold it together and on. I jokingly told the staff it might not be a bad idea to have padlocks on the brace instead of Velcro. I happened to be in the room when the technician measured Jamie for it, and it was interesting to watch. He couldn't move her around much, so it amazed me that he was able to get enough information. He would then call the measurements in to a lab where a computer would "design" the shell based on what had been programmed into it. There were so many things, such as the surgery itself that I found fascinating as well as scary. So many times we go through life not thinking about all the technology, medical and otherwise, that's around us every day. Sometimes we take it for granted, sometimes we don't even know it exists—until the life of someone we love depends on it.

Jamie started Saturday the twelfth still in ICU. She was running a slight fever that morning, so they ran some tests to see if they could find the source of it. They also did an ultrasound of her legs to check for blood clots. Clots can form after periods of inactivity, and the nature of Jamie's injury compounded that possibility. In order to make sure the ultrasound equipment worked properly, a fair amount of pressure had to be put on Jamie's legs. The anti-seizure medication was helping some for the ultra-sensitivity in her legs, but it was obviously still painful when the test was being done. Most of the time when she was moved around for bed linen changing, tests of one shape or form, or examinations, Jamie handled the pain with a "stone-faced smile." That wasn't the case when they pushed on her legs for the ultrasound. There wasn't a smile, but there weren't any complaints either. I know it must have been pretty painful because she hit the self-medicating "pain button" pretty good after that. Shortly after repeatedly hitting the button, Jamie went and sat on a nice sandy beach somewhere, or at least she thought she did.

I have no idea how it got made so fast, but the "turtle shell" that was specially designed for Jamie was delivered Saturday afternoon. That completely blew me away since they had just measured her for it the day before. The chest tube was still in place, so the brace was going to have to wait. That didn't hurt Jamie's feelings any because she wasn't looking forward to wearing it. She had been told she would be wearing it for several months to support and protect her back, as well as to protect the area where the rib had been removed. The results of the ultrasound of her legs showed there weren't any clots, but they put inflatable cuffs on her legs anyway to help minimize the chance of any clots developing. The cuffs would inflate and deflate on a regular basis to help keep blood flowing properly through her legs, thereby helping prevent clots.

Jamie was starting to be a little more aware and conscientious of what she looked like. I thought she looked just fine, but whenever family members would come to her room to visit, she apologized for looking like what she called "a grease ball." She wasn't happy that her hair hadn't been washed since sometime on Tuesday, and she wasn't happy about not having any makeup on. Eric had helped her brush her teeth earlier in the day, which was a good start, but she really wanted her hair washed. Well, later that day she got her wish. I wasn't sure how they were going to manage to do that since she wasn't able to leave her bed and could only be moved a limited amount. I will be the first to admit that I sometimes find the simple things in life fascinating. Maybe it's because of everything that has happened over the years that I have decided life's too short to not appreciate as much as you can, for as long as you can, no matter how "simple" it is. Whatever the reason, I found it interesting how they washed her hair. The nurse laid the bed as flat as possible and placed Jamie's head in an oval-shaped plastic tray. The tray came to a point on one end and had a ledge all the way around it except for where it came to a point. The ledge was a little shorter where it went under Jamie's neck to make it more comfortable. The end opposite the point was elevated slightly, with a bucket placed on the floor under the point to catch the water and shampoo. Some water, some "grease-ball-be-gone," and Jamie had the biggest smile on her face you could imagine. The simple things in life can bring so much pleasure. The greatest pleasure I'd had for some time was seeing the smile on Jamie's face from one of those simple things. And there was nothing "stone-faced" about this smile.

Saturday continued to be a good day for Jamie because she was released from ICU in the late evening. She was moved to a semi-private room with two other ladies. We were told she would be there for a week or so and then would be moving to a rehabilitation wing. The move really tired her out. While she didn't have to do much herself for the move, I think the stress of the whole situation, plus the injuries themselves, took their toll. It only took one bed to get Jamie moved, but it took a couple of carts to move all the flowers, cards, and gifts that had been sent. Only immediate family had been allowed to visit up to that point, but that didn't stop other people from sending cards or gifts. It was amazing how much stuff had accumulated in such a short period. Just as had happened after Stormi's accident, the news of Jamie getting hurt had spread like wildfire. Once again I was greeted by people out of concern for one of my children. And once again, I was deeply honored that one of my children had made enough of a positive impact in her corner of the world that people would stop me to talk out of concern for my child. We updated the Caring Bridge website multiple times a day for the first while, and many people kept track of Jamie's progress that way.

As I said before, Jamie had been saying "thank you" to the nurses each time they gave her a shot. She changed that routine a little bit as soon as she got to her new room. She was getting daily shots in her abdomen area to help prevent blood clots, and there had been talk that she would have to continue receiving those shots even after she was discharged from the hospital. When the nurse came into the room to give her the shot, Jamie asked if she could give it to herself. While she didn't give herself every shot after that, it was the first of many times to come that she did. I didn't remember it at first, but Eric reminded me that Jamie usually gets sick at the sight of a needle. Jamie was taking "baby steps" even without walking.

Jamie's first night in her new room was a restless one. Three people sharing a room meant more doctors, nurses, medical equipment, and so forth—in other words, more noise and commotion. It all added up to Jamie not sleeping well that night. Jamie sent her mom a text the next morning telling her about the restless night she'd had. As the day progressed, Jamie would give Eric a hard time each time her phone wasn't within arm's reach, even if he wasn't the one who had moved it. It was nice to see Jamie starting to get some of her spunk back.

Jamie started receiving diuretics on Sunday, her first day out of ICU, which would help her lose some fluids. Her feet and hands were starting to swell a little from all the IVs she was receiving and from lack of movement. They also started her on pain medication in the form of pills instead of IVs. The IVs were contributing to the fluid buildup, and they said pain medication via IV can start to affect respiratory functions after a period of time. Jamie was doing well with the box she had to blow into to help prevent her lung from collapsing. There continued to be drainage from the chest tube, which meant it would probably have to stay in place for a couple more days. The natural progression from there was that it would be a couple more days before she was able to put the turtle-shell brace on, which meant a couple more days with very limited movement. They also had it planned that someone from the physical therapy department would be coming in on that day to start assessing Jamie and come up with a plan to start working on her legs. That worried me a little because I knew how hypersensitive they still were. But I also knew it had to be done. Whatever extent of walking capabilities Jamie was going to end up with, it was going to take a lot of hard work and pain to get there.

Eric and I kind of watched a football game that afternoon while Jamie was trying to rest. We had the television on, but without any volume. We mostly just sat there looking at the TV. Every once in a while we would say something to each other, but we made sure it was nothing more than a whisper. While Eric and I were doing our best to stay quiet, there was still noise from the other patients. It wasn't that they were trying to make noise, it's just that they had visitors, doctors, and nurses coming and going too. Also, anyone using the restroom had to walk past Jamie's area to get to it. There were curtains that divided each area from the others, and Jamie's area from the restroom, but occasionally one of the curtains would get moved and then left out of place.

Eventually Jamie woke up from her nap and the three of us chatted for a bit. Out of the blue, and while staring straight ahead with a very serious look on her face, Jamie said, "I can't wait until I can stand on my feet." My heart was instantly in my throat. I did my best to say something positive, to say something to the effect that it was going to take some time but that she *would* be standing on them soon enough. While I was trying to figure out what to say next, Jamie said she wanted to be able to stand so she "could fix the 'blankety-blank' curtain that was out of place." Eric knew enough to "volunteer" to fix the curtain and was out of his chair before Jamie had a chance to reopen her mouth. I just shook my head and put my heart back where it belonged. It sure was nice to see Jamie starting to get some of her spunk back.

Monday continued to be more of the same. It was still a game of hurry-up-and-wait in some respects but advancement in others. There wasn't a whole lot that could be done yet in the way of moving. The chest tube was still in, so that meant no turtle shell and no moving around. Dr. Mendez also wanted to be able to take an X-ray of Jamie's back before she would be able to attempt anything major such as walking. In order to take the X-ray, Jamie had to be standing. In order to stand, the chest tube had to be out, and she had to be "stronger." In other words, the X-ray was a little ways off yet. Physical therapy was starting to work with Jamie's legs some. Without moving the rest of her body, she would have to lift her legs up off of the bed and hold them there for a period of time. She would also have to try to flex her feet at the ankles. None of it was easy and it was painful to do, but Jamie tried as hard as she could while keeping a smile on her face, a positive attitude, a sense of humor, and a "please" and "thank you" for anyone who was near her. Jamie was happy that hair washing and sponge baths were going to be part of her daily routine moving forward. It made her feel better about herself, and made the "grease-ball" feeling go away. She was able to put some makeup on, and someone even brought her a daisy to put in her hair. It's amazing how much difference feeling good about your appearance can make. Monday was also the day Jamie was first allowed to have solid food again instead of being "fed" via IV. While that made Jamie very happy, her stomach wasn't so thrilled about it at first. I remember very well from my own accident just how that felt.

Tuesday was a big day for Jamie because the drainage tube came out. Dr. Mendez removed the tube. He said that because the tube was now out, physical therapy would be stopping by later in the day to put the turtle shell on her for the first time. He also said he thought the X-ray of her back would be a week or so away yet. He reiterated that she needed to be standing for the X-ray, which would require the ultra-sensitivity in her legs and feet to have diminished, as well as having some more strength in her legs. Jamie cried when she heard that. It's the one and only time I saw her cry, from the time I talked to her on the phone the day she got hurt, until well past the time she went home. I'm sure she cried other times when I wasn't around, but it was the only time I saw it happen.

Dr. Mendez reassured her that she would walk again, that it was just going to take some time. He reminded her that it easily could have much worse; she could have been paralyzed with no chance of ever being able to walk again, and/or the blow to her head alone could have killed her. I know Jamie understood those scenarios, but it still had to be so hard for her. She had always been such an active person, and now she had to be wondering what kind of activities she was going to be able to do. I can't even imagine how she was feeling, all the things she must have been thinking. I did my best to keep a "stiff upper lip" when she got emotional and while the doctor was talking, but it wasn't easy. I am not one who is usually at a loss for words, but it was getting harder and harder to come up with the right thing to say, or at least what I thought the right thing to say was. I tried to put myself in her place, what I would want to hear that could possibly make me feel better if I was in that situation. I think that made it worse because I couldn't come up with anything that would take away the fear of the unknown for me.

Dr. Mendez left Jamie's room. I gave her a hug and a "daddy kiss," told her how much I loved her and how proud I was of her, and I walked down the hallway. I found the first unoccupied bathroom, went inside, and cried like a newborn. I'd had enough. I had buried my mother because of knee surgery, I had buried my youngest child, and now not even four years later my only other child was hurting, facing an uncertain future, and was scared. I could take no more.

About an hour after the chest tube had been removed, the physical therapy people came in and put the turtle shell on Jamie for the first time. To say it was a painful process would be huge understatement. Before they could put the shell on her, Jamie had to be wearing something besides the standard hospital "peek-a-butt gown." They dressed her in a tight-fitting sleeveless shirt and a pair of shorts. Once she was dressed, she was rolled onto her side. While on her side, they held the back half of the shell against her back, sliding the side of it under her side as much as possible. Jamie was then rolled onto her back with the shell now under her. The pain of the removed rib, the surgery, and her broken back was excruciating at this point, but Jamie continued on. They had to "fine tune" the placement of the back half a little, and then she was ready to have the front put on. After the front was Velcro strapped to the back, it was time for the big test: sitting up. Jamie was given a few moments to rest and then it was time. She was rolled onto her side again and her feet were swung over the edge of the bed. Everything was done in a gentle, semi-slow motion manner, of course. Jamie was then helped into a sitting position. It was extremely painful and she got dizzy, but she sat there for a few minutes with her feet resting on the floor while having help to stay balanced. After she had sat for as long as she could, she was laid back down and the brace was taken off again. Jamie did some leg exercises once she was lying down again, and then it was nap time because she was totally exhausted.

It was decided that Jamie's physical therapy schedule was going to be therapy two times a day. Therapy sessions were going to consist of wearing the shell for an hour each time, sitting up for progressively longer periods of time each session, and continued exercising of her legs. That was about the extent of what she could do until the X-ray of her back had been taken and they felt confident that everything was in its proper place.

While it was easy to be "down" because of what had happened, we also knew there were people who were in much worse situations than what Jamie was in. While Jamie was in ICU, we met the families of two men who were just such people. One of the men was "John." John was a farmer who was injured in an accident involving a tractor. While driving the tractor with a large bale of hay on a loader on the front of the tractor, the tractor hit a bump and the hay bale fell off the loader, landing on John. John's spine was crushed and his neck was broke. He needed surgery to repair as much damage as possible, but they couldn't operate yet due to swelling. At the time we met his family, John had already been waiting three weeks for the surgery and had at least one more week to wait. It was already known that John was paralyzed from the chest down with no chance of there ever being any change or improvement.

The other man's situation was even worse. "Ted" had been working on a porch with a friend. He was only three or four feet off the ground on a short ladder when he leaned over to reach for something. The ladder kicked out and Ted fell, landing on his head. Even though he fell a short distance, Ted broke his neck. While Ted suffered no head injuries and was mentally the same as he had always been, his neck was broke so severely that he was completely paralyzed and would be on a ventilator for the rest of his life. When all of the options were explained to him and his family, Ted decided to have the ventilator removed. Without the ventilator, Ted survived only a matter of a couple of minutes. So many times we go through life thinking we have it rough or feeling sorry for ourselves. More times than not there is someone who is in a worse situation than what we are facing ourselves. I think for the most part Jamie understood that. While it wasn't possible to be "up" all the time, she did a great job keeping a smile on her face, a positive attitude, being grateful for what she had, and using some laughter to get her through the rough spots.

Speaking of laughter, here's an entry Eric wrote for Jamie's Caring Bridge website:

One of Jamie's roommates, "Jean," is an older lady, in her eighties I believe. At one point I had told Jean if she needed anything, like water or something she couldn't reach, to just let me know because I'm right here, and sometimes it's easier than waiting for a nurse.

Yesterday Jean was up and in her chair and I started chatting with her a little. She asked about Jamie. I let her know that Jamie is my girlfriend. Jean asked if she was in a car accident, and I said no, she is a sleepwalker and walked out our patio door. Her eyes got real big and she said, "Oh no," with a look of shock. She made a couple of comments that didn't really make any sense to me, but as Jamie taught me I just smiled and nodded.

Jean was transferred to a nursing home last night, and a few hours after that Jamie's evening nurse came in to do vitals with a big smile on her face and chuckling. She asked if I had been talking to Jean, and I said yeah. The nurse then replied that Jean must have misheard me, because once they had wheeled her out she was just astonished and was telling the PCAs who were taking her out that her roommate was a "*street walker*." So our little Jamie is now a prostitute in the eyes of some little old lady in a nursing home, who will forever be telling stories how she shared a room with a street walker.

Thursday was much the same as the other days as far as physical therapy goes. The day consisted of wearing the back brace as much as possible and doing her leg exercises. In the morning a hospital social worker came in and explained how the rehab process was going to work. There would be occupational and speech therapy as well as the physical therapy. Obviously Jamie needed help with her physical issues, but she also needed to be assessed for any mental issues that may have been caused by the blow to her head and the brain bleeds. And there was the emotional side that needed to be looked at. Whatever her "end results" were going to be as far as having any physical limitations, it could take years before they were fully known. And regardless of what those end results were going to be, Jamie wouldn't be leaving the hospital in the same condition she'd been in when I saw her at work on September 8. She would, however, be leaving the hospital in much better condition than she was when she'd arrived here on September 9.

Jamie did her best to conceal it, but she was understandably scared to leave the surroundings of the hospital. Everything was going to be different now, from the time she woke up in the morning until she went to sleep at night. So many things that used to be easy to do were now going to be a struggle. She had been so active and ran regularly—was she going to be able to do that again? Soon? Ever? Of course before running could be talked about she had to be able to walk. She was also concerned about everyday things like cooking, cleaning, and eventually going back to work. There was understandably a lot on her mind, and the hospital recognized that emotional issues needed to be addressed also.

Even though her future had a lot of uncertainty in it, Jamie's attitude remained great. She kept her smile available at all times, was always polite enough for two people, and remained the "silly" Jamie who loved to laugh. When the social worker told her that an occupational therapist would be in to check on her mental status, Jamie jokingly said, "What are they going to do, ask me a bunch of questions like what's my name and who's the president?" I was there when the occupational therapist came in and I don't remember the therapist asking those two questions, but Jamie wasn't far off. The "test" included a lot of questions that involved memory and also included some drawing and writing. The test went pretty well until it got to the math portion. When the therapist said she was going to start the math portion, Eric and I looked at each other, got big smiles on our faces, and covered our mouths. The therapist looked at us and said, "No helping." It was obviously easier for Eric and me to "take" the math portion because we weren't the ones who were on the "hot seat" or who had fractured his skull.

When the test was done, Jamie said, "Well, aside from that math stuff, I think I did pretty darn well."

The therapist then asked, "Yeah, have you always had problems with math?"

Jamie's immediate response was, "Well, isn't that what a calculator is for anyway?"

Eric and I couldn't contain our laughter anymore and told the therapist that the math portion of the test wouldn't have gone any differently before her fall.

Jamie's response was typical Jamie. She used laughter to try to make light of a situation she was uncomfortable with or scared of. As Eric said, her "math skills" weren't the reason for loving Jamie.

On Wednesday I had started going back to work on a more regular basis, so I felt fortunate to have been there when the occupational therapist came in. While I had to go back to work, I certainly would have rather stayed at Jamie's side. I felt like I was missing out on watching my little girl grow up. I'd missed out in a big way on Friday because Jamie *walked* for the first time since her accident. Dr. Mendez had come in the morning and given Jamie the "green light" to try to stand with assistance and move from her bed to a chair or wheelchair. The doctor knew Jamie had concerns about being able to put the amount of pressure on her feet required to stand, so he asked her to trust him for a test. He said, "I'm going to squeeze your feet really hard and it's not going to hurt, okay?" With a slight look of fear on her face Jamie gave him the green light. He took her feet in his hands and started to squeeze. It was gentle at first, but he started to squeeze harder and harder. Her reaction didn't change any from when he first started to squeeze them gently until he was done squeezing them hard. Dr. Mendez then explained that because of the nerve damage, it's normal for bumps and soft touches to hurt as much or worse than heavy, steady pressure. He added that while he had given her the green light to start working on getting out of bed and getting to a chair, he thought it could be up to two months before she was ready to start walking with a walker. Apparently Jamie didn't like the sound of waiting up to two months to walk and had possibly gained some confidence by having her feet squeezed, because an hour or so after Dr. Mendez left the room she asked for a walker. She was assisted to her feet by two nurses and then took the walker in her hands and took several steps out before turning around and coming back to the bed. I can't even imagine the smile on her face and the pride that was in her heart when she did that. But then again maybe I can, because I know that's how I looked and felt after I got off the phone with her when she called to tell me what she had done.

I don't know if it was a direct result of Jamie taking her first steps on Friday or not, but on Saturday she was moved to the rehabilitation wing of the hospital. I'm sure her first steps at least gave the hospital staff the insight that Jamie was ready for challenges that were ahead of her. Saturday was also the day she got to go outside for the first time since she'd been injured. Jamie was understandably very excited about that. Eric gave her a ride around the hospital grounds in a wheelchair.

My work schedule didn't allow me to make it to the hospital on Saturday, but I made it there on Sunday and it's a day I will *never* forget. When my fiancée, Robyn, and I got to the hospital, Jamie and Eric were sitting in the family area of the rehab wing watching the start of a Vikings football game. Jamie looked absolutely beautiful. She was so much happier now that she was able to dress up a little more and wear makeup. Of course whatever she wore, her turtle shell was going to be covering some of it, but at least she was wearing something that made her feel better about her appearance than a hospital gown. We sat and talked for a while, and part of the conversation was about how cold some of the people there felt sitting in the family area. Jamie started heading toward her room in her wheelchair and wouldn't allow anyone to go with her. She returned a few minutes later with some blankets for those who were cold. She's recovering from a near-death accident, and she's worried about other people. That's my Jamie.

A little later on, Jamie was sitting on the edge of her bed after eating her dinner and asked me if I would like to watch her walk. I asked her if she would like to watch me cry. We both said, "Sure."

With a little help from me, she stood up from the edge of the bed, took hold of her walker, and headed out the door of her room toward the family area. It wasn't the fastest I had ever seen her walk, but it was by far the "best" I have ever seen her walk. It was all my hopes and dreams of the nine days prior to that, combined into a sixty-foot walk.

I thought back to the first time Jamie ever walked. As great a moment as that was, this one was so much better. What Ma Sue had said when she heard me talk for the first time after the bull attacked me was so very true: "Sometimes the *second* first time is way more special than the *first* first time." If only Ma Sue had known how those words would ring true for me thirty-four years later. I did a good job keeping my composure while watching Jamie walk, limiting my crying to just wet eyes. She had seen me cry enough in the nine days prior—actually, the four years prior—I didn't want her to think I was still crying "sad" tears. I couldn't have been any happier or more proud of her. I walked with her to the family area and excused myself to use a restroom. I walked down the hallway, found an unoccupied restroom, and . . . I think you know what happened next. At least this time they were happy tears. I also fired off another round of a thousand prayers while I was in there. This time I was saying "thank you" instead of "please." Jamie's manners were starting to rub off on me.

We sat and talked for a while and at some point Jamie decided to be silly and get everyone to laugh. She was sitting on a two-person bench and she leaned back against one of the arms of the bench. She then pulled her walker on top of herself, put her arms out like she had fallen and was struggling to get her balance, and then added the finishing touch of pulling a face to make it seem "real." Besides making us nervous that she was going to hurt herself—worse, she also made us all laugh. We took pictures of course and added them to her Caring Bridge website.

Jamie laughed at herself a lot to get through some of the rough spots, both in the hospital and after returning home. Whether she was consciously doing it or not, I don't know, but ultimately she was helping herself heal when she laughed. Both laughing and crying can be very important tools in the healing process, and while it's not always possible or practical, everyone knows that laughing is more fun than crying. I know Jamie cried more than the one time I saw, but I saw her laugh *many* times. In my mind, Jamie used "LAUGHTER" to help get herself through: Laughing Again Ultimately Gains Healing as The End Result.

Jamie couldn't "laugh her way" through everything that came along or happened; nobody could or can. Laughing can't heal physical injuries, but neither can crying. Laughing, as well as crying, can however help heal emotional injuries. I think most everyone would agree that having emotional injuries healed, or in the process of healing, will go a long way toward helping physical injuries heal. Not all physical injuries can be healed, not all emotional injuries can be healed, but having a good attitude is key to helping the healing process go as far as it can. From what I could tell, Jamie was doing a great job of using LAUGHTER to get where she was going.

The next almost-two weeks were a real test for Jamie. Each day required a little more of her in terms of physical work. She had therapy sessions for a good portion of each day, and it wasn't just physical therapy, it was speech and occupational therapy as well. Speech therapy wasn't necessarily just for talking, occupational therapy wasn't necessarily just job related; they were for helping prepare Jamie in every way to go home. They had to make sure she was emotionally ready to go home. They had to make sure she was able to dress herself. She had to be able to navigate around a kitchen in a safe manner, including being able to handle hot pots and pans while using a walker. The therapy department even had a kitchen, and before Jamie would be allowed to go home she had to cook a complete meal for the therapist, right down to making the grocery list for the meal. She had to be able to navigate safely up and down stairs. In other words, there was a lot to accomplish. While I don't remember there ever being any kind of schedule of when she needed to accomplish each level, she was pushed hard to get to the next level. At one point, Jamie said it seemed like they were asking her to walk twenty feet with a walker one day and asking her to walk unassisted the next. I happened to be sitting in on the therapy session when she walked for the first time without a walker. Jamie had a belt around her waist that the therapist held on to as Jamie took a few steps. The look of sheer terror on Jamie's face was soon replaced with that great big beautiful smile of hers.

As she progressed through the therapy department, Jamie also progressed into a different room on the rehab floor. It was room that offered her a little more independence. It had a larger bed that was more like one at home instead of like a hospital bed. It had a larger shower so she was able to work up to showering without assistance.

I was amazed at how far she'd progressed in a short period of time. The therapy people did a wonderful job of working with and teaching Jamie. But ultimately, it was because of her hard work and determination that Jamie progressed as far and as quickly as she did. Her hard work didn't come without a price though. When she wasn't in therapy, she was sleeping. When a person's body goes through major trauma such as Jamie's, it's only natural for the person to be extra tired from injury itself, besides from the person's body trying to heal. Plus everything she did now required extra effort. It was harder for her to walk and it required extra effort to move about with the turtle shell on. On top of all of that, she had several therapy sessions each day. It all added up to Jamie being very tired a good portion of the time, which was about as frustrating as anything for her. I gave her a few talks, hugs, and daddy kisses trying to reassure her it could only get better.

Of course there were things at home that needed to be addressed. Securing the patio door Jamie had walked out of was taken care, but that was only a small portion of the issue. No one could say for certain one way or the other, but chances were that Jamie was going to continue to sleepwalk. If that was the case, securing the patio door would do nothing to protect her from all the other hazards that each and every home has. Stairs, stoves, kitchen utensils, all the things Jamie had used while sleepwalking in the past. Locking the bedroom door wasn't an option because of the danger of having to try to find a key in case of fire. Plus, if Jamie knew where the key was, there was always the potential that she would be able to open the door while sleepwalking anyway. The decision was made to put an alarm on the bedroom door. I knew Jamie was as safe there as anywhere, but I wanted her to be my "little girl" again and live with me.

At long last, on September 30, twenty-one days after she was injured, Jamie was released from the hospital. What a marvelous, miraculous event. What a simply terrifying event. There was a meeting before Jamie was released between some of the therapists who had worked with Jamie, some of the doctors who had provided her care, her family, and of course Jamie herself. We were reminded again how fortunate she was to be able to walk. We were reminded again how fortunate she was not to have any major issues due to the skull fracture and brain bleeds. They outlined for us where she had started from and where she now was, at that time. They also told us "where she would be going" from there. There would be numerous doctor visits for a while as well as therapy sessions. What they didn't or couldn't tell us was what her end results were going to be. Would her walk become normal? If it did, would she then be able to run again? Would her "bathroom control issues" resolve themselves? Questions neither they nor anyone could answer. But one thing was certain—Jamie was going home. While fear of the unknown was somewhat terrifying, it was vastly overshadowed by the fact that Jamie was leaving that hospital and going home to a house on a rolling hillside in rural Wisconsin, instead of going home to a house on Heavenly Isle Drive. What a marvelous, miraculous event . . .

Jamie took a couple days "off" once she got home, but then it was right back to physical therapy sessions to help her gain more strength and see if they could get her walk to improve. Because of the nerve damage in her spinal cord, the "fronts" of her feet weren't lifting up when she walked like they normally would. It was several months before she was allowed to drive, so I took Jamie to a few of her therapy sessions. Before she would be allowed to drive Jamie had to be done wearing the turtle brace, as well as the soft-shell one that followed, she had to have a better range of motion in her upper body, and she had to have better control of her feet.

I saw the coolest thing at one of the sessions I took Jamie to. The therapist was trying to determine how well the nerve connection between Jamie's back and feet was working. They were using a small electrical device that sent out small "pulses" of electricity similar to what a person's nervous system does. They had one wire attached to Jamie's leg just above her knee, and the other was attached just above her ankle. When they sent an electrical pulse through the wires, nothing happened. The therapist wasn't sure if the lower wire was in the proper place or not, so he took it off of Jamie and attached it to the back of his hand. He then turned the machine on and ran his "pointer" finger around that area until *he* felt a tingle of electricity. He carefully marked the exact spot where he had felt the tingle and reattached the wire to Jamie in that spot. He then turned the machine back on, and Jamie's foot lifted right up. The look on her face when her foot lifted up was priceless.

There were many more therapy sessions and numerous doctor visits. Jamie saw Dr. Mendez (Dr. Magic Fingers, as Eric called him) a few times as well as an urologist. Dr. Mendez said Jamie was healing as well as could be expected. He said the greatest amount of improvement would be seen in the first six to nine months. After a year's time, he said, there wouldn't be much chance of improvement. Jamie had to continue to work hard at making improvements, but she was only going to be able to go as far as her body and injuries would allow. I knew Jamie continuing to work hard wouldn't be a problem. Jamie also had a number of appointments with an urologist. Just as Dr. Mendez had said in the emergency room might happen after shattering the particular vertebra she did, Jamie had some "control" issues. Her bladder didn't always empty completely and sometimes emptied when it wasn't supposed to. As a result, Jamie ended up with a number of urinary tract infections, and was nervous about venturing too far from a restroom. Even though she was dealing with a lot of hardships, Jamie still did a wonderful job keeping a positive attitude, keeping a smile on her face, and laughing as much as possible. I can't begin to tell you how proud I was of her.

It was starting to become apparent that Jamie was going to have some permanent disabilities. From what I could tell, she was handling it pretty well. I was thankful for many things, including the fact that I still had her, but I was also thankful for some other things. I was thankful for some of the trips I had taken with the girls over the years and some of the things we had done while on those trips, things that Jamie wouldn't now be able to do. I was also thankful Jamie and I had gone to Africa with Dad in July 2007. We were there for two weeks helping build a nursery school for an orphanage. What an incredible experience. The people there have so little and we have so much. Jamie mentioned that trip to me a couple of times while she was in the hospital, and how much she had to be thankful for. What unselfish insight. I am very thankful I got to spend that time with Jamie, and Dad, because it's not likely she could physically do that now. Jamie also went skydiving about a month before her accident. She said she had a blast. And again, it's not something she could likely do again.

In May 2010 Jamie and I walked together for a 5K run, a run she had "ran" the year before. Jamie walked with walking poles just in case she lost her balance, but she never lost her balance and only used them for stability. She was asked at the halfway point if she wanted to stop and take a break, but Jamie refused and kept going. There were a lot of cheers and pictures taken at the finish line. There was a lot of pride also. It was by no means the way Jamie wanted to be participating in the race, but she took it in stride and did it with a smile on her face. I had a huge smile on my face too. It was great seeing her out and about, but the fact that she was able walk that whole distance without stopping was incredible. It was great practice for walking her down the aisle someday.

In August 2011, Jamie had a "pacemaker" implanted that was designed to help her bladder empty more completely and regularly. It has helped to some degree, but not to the extent that was hoped for. She still occasionally gets a urinary tract infection and doesn't like to stray too far from a restroom. About that same time, Jamie decided she wanted to be "med free" and quit taking the medication she had been on to help control the tingling and pain in her feet. She said there is discomfort now when she walks, but it's tolerable. The front of Jamie's feet never did get to the point where they lift up while walking like they did before. As a result, she walks with what I call "a cute little shuffle." Also as a result of her feet not working the way they used to, she easily gets out of balance and occasionally takes a tumble because of it, especially in slippery conditions such as a shower or when walking on ice. While her long-term memory is fine, she does suffer some short-term memory loss. While these issues might keep some people down, it doesn't keep Jamie down. She still exercises regularly and even rides a bike, and I don't mean a stationary one. It worries me when she rides it back and forth to work, but Jamie keeps telling me she will be fine. Because of her balance not being what it once was, Jamie can't work as a server anymore, but she still works part time as a hostess. Not being lazy in any way, shape, or form, Jamie basically works seven days a week between her two jobs.

When Jamie got home from the hospital, she started a "blessings jar" and put a note in it each day listing something she was thankful for. She still goes outside most every night when the stars are shining and looks up at the heavens, giving thanks for what she has. And she takes a look to see if she can "find" Ma Sue and Stormi.

In late 2011, the relationship between Jamie and Eric came to an end. They remain close friends, and Jamie still works for Eric. When Jamie told me the news of the breakup, I thought back to how I felt when seeing them together at the hospital. I thought about the countless hours Eric spent at the hospital and at home caring for Jamie. I can only hope and pray that the man Jamie marries someday will treat her with the same kindness, respect, patience of her physical limitations, and love that Eric did. Thank you, Eric.

After Ma Sue and Stormi died, I thought I had learned everything I was ever going to learn about grief. And I thought that grieving was always associated with death. I was way wrong on both accounts. I quickly learned that you can also grieve for someone who is hurting. I quickly learned that you can grieve for someone who is scared. I grieve when Jamie tells me she fell in the shower, or on ice, again. I grieve when I see the pain in her eyes from a urinary tract infection. I grieve when she tells me she can't remember something. I grieve when I see a "flash" of sadness in her eyes when she sees someone out running. I grieve when I see her walking and lose her balance because of something most people would have no trouble with. I do my best to never let Jamie see my grief. It's not that I feel sorry for her when I grieve; Jamie would never accept that. I just want her body to be whole and normal like it used to be. I don't want that for me, I want that for her. Through it all, Jamie does a wonderful job keeping a smile on her face and a positive attitude. There are down moments or days, but she doesn't allow herself to stay down. It usually doesn't take long and she is laughing again.

I can't begin to tell you how proud I am of Jamie. She has taught me so much about being strong. She has taught me so much about the importance of smiling and laughter. She has taught me so much about appreciating what we have and living every day to the fullest. She taught me that if you're going to say "please," you also have to say "thank you."

I will close this by repeating something I said to Jamie when she was about to be released from the hospital: "Jamie, when I grow up, I want to be just like you. I couldn't possibly love you any more than I do.

Love,
Dad."

*   *   *

Have you ever finished Christmas shopping for your kids and then looked at the pile of gifts you bought for each of them and thought you'd somehow made a mistake because one pile of gifts appeared to be larger than the other? The thought of things not being "even" bothered you because the same amount of thought, time, energy, love, and even money had gone into the gifts for both kids.

That's how I feel when I look at what I have written for Stormi and Jamie. While it wasn't anything I bought for them, the same amount of thought, time, energy, and love went into what I wrote for each of the girls. And yet the pile of papers on the floor for Stormi's section of the book appeared to be larger than Jamie's.

The more I thought about it, the more it made sense that things didn't appear even. For one thing, Stormi's "journey" is complete, but Jamie's isn't. A lot of what I wrote about Stormi was dealing with her accident, making of arrangements, her visitation, her funeral, and dealing with grief. Writing about Jamie's accident along with her recovery didn't require as many words or pages. The other big reason I see for the unevenness is that it takes more to explain a person's thoughts on grief than it does to explain their thoughts on joy. If you think about it, people tend to "talk" more about their feelings if they are feeling down than they do if they are feeling on top of the world.

I have tried, and I have tried hard, to be mad at God for what happened to Ma Sue, Stormi, and Jamie. But I just can't. It's not his fault. We do not exist on this earth as "puppets" in a "puppet show" with God as the "Puppet Master." We are free to do what we want, when we want. We are free to have our own thoughts. The very fact that I am writing my thoughts down in this book proves that. We don't have "strings" attached to us controlling our every move. Because this life is not a controlled situation, it is not a perfect situation and things are going to happen. Some of the things will be good, some bad. I know life doesn't work on a system of "heaven points," but how is it right that Ma Sue died from complications of surgery while getting ready for a *mission* trip? How is it right that Stormi died at the age of only eighteen? How is it right that Jamie was injured and permanently disabled at age twenty-four? Again, life is not a puppet show. If it was, it would be a perfect life and no one would ever get sick or hurt, but that's not how it works. God doesn't cause things to happen as a puppet master does, he just allows things to happen, good or bad. I believe God knows ahead of time what's going to happen, and one might say, "Why doesn't he intervene and stop the bad from happening?" If he did intervene, then we're back to being puppets, which we're not. It's up to us humans to take care of ourselves and each other as much as possible.

Even though I've decided I'm not mad at God for what happened to Ma Sue, Stormi, and Jamie, there have been many times since 2005 that I have wondered why I was allowed to survive my accident only to feel the pain of what had happened to the girls and Ma Sue. I find it so unfair in many ways. I even feel guilty about it in some ways. But it's the way it is, and neither I nor anyone else can change it. I have to be thankful for the time I had with Ma Sue and Stormi, and be thankful I still have Jamie. I have to do the best I can and work through the rough spots in life.

Going through some of life's rough spots, I like to take the **LIFE WINS** approach: **L**iving **I**n-spite of **F**ateful **E**vents **W**ondrously **I**nspires **N**ew **S**uccess.

When I say "living," I mean carrying on with life after a fateful event and doing the best we can in-spite of a fateful situation. As I said before, Stormi wouldn't just want me to carry on, she would expect me to. I know Ma Sue would feel the same way. I am of no use to myself or anyone else if I decide to stop living because of fateful events. When I say "success," I don't necessarily mean to become successful in the business world, or that our pocketbooks will be full. I mean we will have success in our hearts, and our hearts will be full. I am trying to live the kind of life Ma Sue would be proud of. Because Stormi isn't able to accomplish the good things in life she would have done, I will do my best to accomplish some good *for* her. I will try my hardest to be the best dad possible for Jamie. Even though she taught me about strength, I will be there and be strong for Jamie should she need it. The way I see it, if I can continue living in that manner, then I will have success beyond my wildest dreams. We can't always control the bad things that happen in life, but most times we can control how we respond to those bad things, those fateful events. If we have a good attitude, put a smile on our face, and try our best, we will wondrously inspire our own hearts, and possibly others' as well, to be successful.

I have had an interesting and sometimes challenging life to this point. In my eyes, some of it has been more than fair, some of it has been very unfair. But the way I see it, if I can keep my **CHIN UP** and use some **LAUGHTER** along the way, then ultimately **LIFE WINS**.